Praise for *Bank on Yourself*

"Harrison and McCormick provide an extremely thorough and uniquely insightful exploration of financial planning, and financial decision making, from a woman's perspective. *Bank on Yourself* teaches the importance and power of financial literacy, and the role it can play in building confidence and financial security. To get you started successfully on your own personal financial journey, the book is filled with many first-hand examples and worksheets, from women of all ages and experience. This book is a fabulous financial guide for women of all ages and circumstances because there is no more important principle to learn in your life than the power and confidence that comes from Banking on Yourself."

—Douglas V. Nelson, President, Nelson Financial Consultants, and author of *Master Your Retirement: How to Fulfill Your Dreams with Peace of Mind*

"This book is full of great and, may I say, vital information for women of all ages and stages of life. Great work! It's time we have this information in a format that we can understand, and that will encourage us to take charge of our financial wealth."

—Sandra Rinomato, Real Estate Broker, Television Host and Author

"The authors tailor their advice to women at all life stages, using their own experiences as a guide. I like their idea of writing a motto to motivate you, using words such as family and friends, adventure and charity. Combining the motto with a vision for your future will give you the confidence to make good financial decisions."

—Ellen Roseman, *Toronto Star* personal finance columnist and continuing education instructor

"It's a fact of life that we all enter this world as singles and will most likely exit it in the same state, no matter how many happy decades some couples may enjoy. Ardelle Harrison is the template for a single woman who created her own financial independence outside the realm of coupledom; and financial advisor Leslie McCormick has plenty of experience counselling women how to plan financially to be single, even if they are not currently on their own."

—Jonathan Chevreau, Publisher of the Financial Independence Hub, author of *Findependence Day* and co-author of *Victory Lap Retirement*

BANK

ON

Yourself

BANK

ON

Yourself

WHY EVERY WOMAN
SHOULD PLAN FINANCIALLY
TO BE SINGLE,
EVEN IF SHE'S NOT

Ardelle Harrison
Leslie McCormick

MILNER &
ASSOCIATES INC
· EDITING · PUBLISHING · COMMUNICATIONS · CONSULTING

ISBN 978-1-988344-10-2 (paperback)
ISBN 978-1-988344-11-9 (ebook)

Production Credits
Editor and project manager: Karen Milner
Copy editor: Lindsay Humphreys
Interior design and typesetting: Adrian So, adriansodesign.com
Cover design: Adrian So, adriansodesign.com

Printer: Friesens
Published by Milner & Associates Inc.
www.milnerassociates.ca

Printed in Canada
10 9 8 7 6 5 4 3 2 1

To my former students who inspired me to write this book.

*To my parents who, by example, taught me how to manage money.
I am forever grateful that, because of your planning and saving,
I was financially supported during my undergraduate.*

*And to my other family members, including my many friends who are
my extended family. Thanks to all of you, my life is rich in countless
wonderful ways.*

—AH

*To my parents: For the values you instilled in me, the lessons you
taught me and the encouragement you always provide.*

*To my husband: You supported my career aspirations and supported
me in taking the risk so many years ago to become the advisor I
am today. While our life can be crazy at times, it is certainly a fun
adventure and I am so glad to be sharing it with you. I love you.*

*To my daughters: You are such a blessing to me and you make my life
rich. As you grow into young women, may you make wise decisions
and choices so that you, too, will be able to enjoy a life of true wealth,
where you not only achieve financial independence, but also have the
ability to focus on the relationships, interests and pursuits that bring
you joy.*

*And to my clients: While my role is to help you navigate your
financial journey, I have also learned so much from you. Thank you
for the privilege of working with you and sharing in your lives. It truly
is an honour.*

—LM

CONTENTS

ACKNOWLEDGEMENTS

A very sincere thank you to everyone who agreed to be interviewed and was part of our focus groups. Your willingness to share your stories, life lessons and opinions is greatly appreciated, and your contributions were invaluable to this book.

Being first-time book authors, our learning curve was steep. A special thank you to our families, friends and colleagues for encouraging us to press on, and to those voices of experience who helped guide us forward.

We had an idea and conducted the research then put everything together in written format, all of which was only the beginning phase of our project. Our editor, Karen Milner, is the talent who brought everything together and coordinated her team to produce a professionally finished product. Not only could we rely on her expertise, it was truly a pleasure to work with Karen.

In advance, we thank our readers. May *Bank on Yourself* help you enjoy your journey on the road to financial independence, and may you experience a life of true wealth—one that is not just rich financially, but also rich in all the areas of life that bring you joy.

Chapter 1

ONCE SINGLE, ALWAYS SINGLE, OR SINGLE AGAIN

Every woman should plan financially to be single, even if she is not. Why? The answer is really rather simple: Ninety percent of women will end up managing their own finances at some point during their life due to divorce, widowhood or having never married at all.[1]

Before we get too far, let us be clear. We are not advocating that those of you who are married or in a committed relationship should plan your finances excluding or independent of your partner. Rather, planning for the day you may be single also includes planning *for* each other, to ensure that, if something should happen to one of you, the other will be okay. And shouldn't that be what we want for those we love? Besides, quite frankly, it is safe to say that at least one person in the partnership, most likely the female, will end up single at some point.

According to the 2016 Canadian census, centenarians are the fastest-growing population and there are five females for every one male who is over the age of one hundred. The fact is, we are all living longer and, no matter how long you live, women are outliving men. So, it's important to plan for that statistical probability even if you are part of a couple now.

Secondly, the trend to stay single is growing quickly. Pew Research has predicted that when today's young adults reach their mid-forties and fifties, about 25 percent are likely never to have been married, and history has shown that the chances of marrying for the first time after that age are very small.[2] Whether by choice or by circumstance, the trend to remain single is growing among women.

The reality is, at some point during your life, if not for your whole adult life, you will be solely responsible for your finances. The consequences of not taking responsibility for your financial future are grim, considering that 28.3 percent of unattached seniors live in poverty.[3] In fact, older women living on their own are thirteen times more likely to be poor than seniors living in families.[4] And wealth, or the lack thereof, affects health: living in poverty actually reduces life expectancy.[5] But you have the power to avoid being one of these gloomy statistics, and we are here to show you how.

Not much more than a generation or two ago, women didn't have the opportunities we have today to be in control of our own destiny and our own financial future. Not only has the quality and level of education that women receive increased, females now make up the majority of students graduating from university.[6] In the workforce, virtually any occupation today is open to us. The trailblazers who went before us opened the door to incredible opportunity and the freedom for women to be independent; whether it be fully autonomous or in a partnership, we are able to stand on our own two feet.

Unfortunately, even with the incredible steps forward women have taken, many are not fully prepared or do not feel empowered to realize the financial potential they now have. Some still spend their lives waiting for Mr. Right to come along—someone who will take care of them, including make all their financial dreams possible. Some are in relationships and comfortable financially but may be in the dark about their money matters as a couple. Others are thrust into singlehood by the death of a partner or by separation or divorce and suddenly have to go it alone in an already difficult circumstance. And a growing number of women choose to live their lives independently—happily and intentionally single.

The point is, whether you have ever been single, think you always will be single or are in a situation where you could be single once again, you need to plan financially for life on your own—to feel confident in your financial position, to ensure you have choices and options, and to achieve not only financial security but true financial independence.

We define financial security as having a roof over your head and food on the table; the ability to get by somewhat comfortably without being a burden or being dependent on others financially. But there's more than that to financial independence. Financial independence is not only about being financially secure, it's also about having the freedom to focus on the interests, goals and relationships that bring you joy and fulfillment, without having significant financial concern, both during your working years and, ultimately, during your retirement—whatever that means to you. It's about being comfortable for your lifetime, with work being something you enjoy; and, if work is part of your "retirement," it's because you choose it, not because you *have to* keep working to get by. Financial security may be the basic objective, but financial independence is the higher goal.

There isn't one generic way to achieve financial success. Each person has her own unique situation, challenges, strengths and abilities. We, therefore, cannot give you an exact recipe to follow to guarantee success. What we can do is give you specific tools and practical ideas—as well as many examples of accomplishments and lessons learned from the wonderful women who participated in focus groups as part of research for this book. These women represent all different walks of life, ages, stages and careers. Some are married (or otherwise "coupled up"), some are single again and others have always been single. In addition, we received valuable input from men who want what's best for their wives, partners, daughters and sisters. All of their stories and experiences have contributed to the content of this book for the purpose of helping you achieve financial success your own way.

Securing your financial future and achieving financial independence require not just good planning but also your dedication to making these goals happen. It will be a challenge. There will be sacrifices you will have to make. Financial independence does not come automatically, or even easily; it is up to you to make it happen. You cannot rely on government assistance nor the generosity of others to get you through.

Some people rely on an inheritance as their financial plan, but this kind of windfall should be viewed as a possibility, not a guarantee. Furthermore, it's important to realize that inheritances could be smaller in the future because people are living longer and spending more, not only on enjoying and maintaining an active lifestyle during retirement, but also on health care throughout their extended senior years. A remarriage can also alter the financial landscape, or the unfortunate circumstances of a rift in a relationship can result in a changed will. The bottom line is, inheritances cannot be controlled, nor can they be relied upon to upgrade your own lifestyle.

You certainly can't rely on the ever-elusive lottery win to bring you financial security, even though a disturbing number of people are doing so. The odds of winning the lottery are infinitesimal. It can be fun to dream, and sometimes we feel the need to buy a ticket for the sense of optimism it brings; but at the end of the day, your financial success is up to you. You need to make the choice to make your own lottery actually happen. It takes hard work and smart work, both in the planning and the execution. You must live up to the responsibility for your own financial independence if you want to enjoy the rewards. You don't need to win the lottery; you can create your own luck.

There's no way around it: achieving financial independence is hard work. It's hard work for couples; it's hard work for those who have to "start again" after divorce; it's hard work for those who find themselves widowed and on their own; and it can be even harder to achieve it entirely on one's own, without ever having a spouse or life partner. Yes, it's a huge challenge to live well and plan for the future when you're suddenly or always single, but think of the freedom and the sense of accomplishment you will have from knowing that you are in control of your financial future and that you can and will achieve financial success all on your own. Although it may seem daunting, many women have done it.

This book is written by women who represent the audience it is intended for. Not only will you gain sound professional insight from the extensive experience of a female Senior Wealth Advisor, Leslie, who is a wife and mother of two daughters, you also will learn from Ardelle, a retired woman who has remained single her whole life and managed to reach all her financial goals by herself. We are happy to share our journeys in a personal and supportive way to help and encourage you to move forward and take control of your financial future.

We all need positive influences and good advice so that we can achieve what is possible; we can also learn from our mistakes and the mistakes of others. And so, throughout the book, we'll provide you with cautionary tales; examples of women who have planned successfully for themselves; and sound, practical advice on how you can do the same. No one would voluntarily choose to live in poverty or to have no choice but to work during their senior years out of financial necessity. As mothers, aunts and daughters, we don't want this to happen to us, nor do we want it to happen to our mothers, aunts, daughters or other loved ones. We all want financial success for ourselves and for those we love.

Achieving financial freedom is a journey and it's not always a smooth one, with twists and turns you can't predict. Nevertheless, the destination, financial independence—whether you have always been single, have a partner or are married, or you are single again—is within your reach and worth living up to the challenge. The rest of your journey starts today.

PART 1

RISE TO THE CHALLENGE

Chapter 2

EVEN THOUGH YOU MAY BE SINGLE, YOU ARE NOT ALONE

Every woman has a story, and each of our stories is unique. In your story, you are the leading lady and you have the power to write your own narrative. When you look back on the story of your life, how do you want the chapters to read? Will yours be a tale of strength, of overcoming challenges and of achievement? Will you look back at what you have built—maybe on your own, maybe with the help of a partner—and be proud of what you have accomplished? Will those accomplishments include financial independence—being able to spend your time and resources on those things that bring you joy without being worried about money? Yes, circumstance will play a role, but you are both the main character and the author of your life's work. The choices you make will have far more influence on your story than will luck. Will you choose a happy ending for yourself?

In any story, there are challenges. That's what makes the journey so interesting and rewarding. But as you look to achieve financial independence, there are some common challenges you'll encounter that we all face. There are the practical challenges, such as actually building the amount of wealth you need to finance a comfortable lifestyle in retirement and create sufficient income for your lifetime. Longer life expectancies mean that some people are actually spending more years being retired than they did working! Someone retiring at age sixty, for example, could very well need to finance thirty-plus years ahead of them. And we've already seen that this is a bigger issue for women because we have longer life expectancies than men.

The pressure of inflation is another challenge, no matter what age you are. In order to be financially independent, not only do you need to be able to fund your lifestyle for a long time, you will need to have enough to cover the ever-increasing cost of living. Inflation results in higher prices next year for the same goods and services you may have purchased this year. If you were to spend $150 on groceries today, in twenty years, at a 3-percent inflation rate, those same groceries will cost over $270. As the cost of living increases, it is essential that your income increases along with it if you want to be able to maintain your comfortable lifestyle for your lifetime.

For those who enter retirement married or partnered, there are some distinct financial advantages: potentially two sets of government benefits, two sets of retirement accounts and other investment accounts and/or pensions, as well as the potential to split incomes and save tax. That's two sets of income sources and the ability to reduce what, in Canada, for many people is their single-largest expense over their lifetime—tax. That's great news for married couples. For those who are single, or who find themselves single again, being able to afford to retire comfortably (and remain that way) falls on your own savings, your own government benefits and your own pension, if you have one. You have to do it all yourself, with no tax advantages and, in fact, with a tax disadvantage! There is no opportunity to reduce the taxes on your income through income splitting. Generally speaking, for the same level of household income, a single person pays more tax than a two-person household.

But don't despair! Overcoming these kinds of real, practical challenges is possible if you plan carefully for a future of financial independence. Helping conquer these practical challenges is really what this book is all about. Banking on yourself is about improving your financial knowledge and situation today, as well as building the amount of wealth you need to afford a comfortable lifestyle in retirement and create sufficient income for your lifetime.

BEYOND THE NUMBERS

In order to achieve financial independence, we must also recognize that it isn't about just the numbers, or strategy. We are human, we are social, we have emotions, and these factors also impact our ability to enjoy, or even plan for, a comfortable lifestyle for our lifetime. In fact, some of the hardest challenges to overcome can be our own emotions, especially fear and self-doubt.

As much as the responsibility falls on your shoulders to achieve financial independence, there are also supporting roles that people in your life fill. Some people are positive, some are negative, either propelling us forward or causing us to stumble. Therefore, we must help you develop the right mindset and the willingness to overcome the psychological and emotional challenges as well as the financial ones. To do this, we first need to take a look at some of the non-financial issues that may be holding you back from being financially successful, especially if you are on your own.

SUPPORTING ROLES

If you are currently single (or planning for a time when you may be), you are on your own in most ways and in most things; however, we are all influenced by others. Sometimes that influence is positive, other times it is negative. Regardless of whether the influence is positive or negative, both types can motivate you to reach your goals.

Positive Influences

Positive influences include your cheerleaders—those people who, through thick or thin, will cheer you on and encourage you to be the best you can be. Just like in a marathon, you are the one running the race, but others help you train and provide support, so you can cross the finish line. They may even be helpful by playing devil's advocate. They care enough to help you by asking the tough "What if?" questions, not to dissuade you from your goals, but rather to help make sure your plans are good and solid; that you have thought about the "what ifs" and have a plan to address them if they come to pass. These people challenge you to do your best, so they may push you to a new level and they may not accept excuses. Keep your cheerleaders close. They help propel you forward.

Other positive influences may be those people you look to and think, "Wow! Isn't it amazing what she has done?" Perhaps you are inspired by someone who has overcome a significant challenge or who has achieved phenomenal success in some aspect of life. These people make you think, "If she can do it, so can I!" These positive influences motivate us, build us up and contribute to our confidence. They are great role models and can be our mentors. If you want to be successful, surround yourself with people who have achieved success. Just like a student who will be more likely to do well in school if her friends work hard, you will be more likely to achieve financial success if you associate with others who value financial independence.

Negative Influences

On the other hand, some influences are negative. Expensive friends, for instance. Yes, even though good friends are priceless, they can be pricey. And, let's face it, there will always be other people, including some friends of yours, who will make more money than you do and therefore can afford nicer clothes, a bigger home, a newer car or a more exotic trip. Their influence can be negative if you make the choice to try to live their life instead of living the life you can afford. Keeping up might feel great in the moment, but if you allow yourself to spend beyond your means simply to keep up with someone else, it may be what keeps you from long-term financial success.

Leslie has seen all too often how "keeping up with the Joneses" can be a direct route to regret down the road. In her professional career, she has encountered too many people who chose this path only to arrive on the doorstep of retirement with insufficient assets. In fact, many of these folks, who spent their lives trying to keep up with the lifestyle of others and now face retirement with too much debt and too few assets, somehow expect Leslie to wave a magic wand to make it all work. Unfortunately, the advice that often needs to be given in this circumstance is not what people want to hear. Typically, they must do one or more of the following:

- keep working because they have to

- sell non–income-producing assets (i.e., toys) to buy assets that will produce an income or pay off debt

- sell their home, pay off debt and potentially have to rent

- simplify their lifestyle for the rest of their lifetime

These are not the choices you want to be faced with down the line because you chose to live a life you couldn't afford.

Instead of keeping up with the Joneses, run your own race. Let what *you* value most be your guide to helping you choose what you spend money on and what you don't—don't base your decisions on the priorities of your friends, especially those who have more expensive tastes. Be happy for your friends today, but don't let their choices become your priorities. You never know, those friends who spend liberally may not even be able to afford their own lifestyle. They might actually be trying to keep up with someone else! True friends won't force you to keep up with them; they accept you and your lifestyle. They may even admire your choices.

The key is to know your financial limits, and don't try to keep up to others' lifestyle if it means sacrificing your future. Make sure your older self will thank your younger self for balancing fun today with being smart about tomorrow. Allow yourself to be motivated by the success of those whose lifestyle you admire and aspire to, and let that motivation drive you to build the future you want for yourself.

Be aware that some negative influences can be even more insidious, including those who try to hold you back rather than let you get ahead. You know the ones. They are the people who make you doubt yourself mainly because they are pessimistic, or they don't want you to succeed more than they will, or they wonder why they're not able to go after the same goals. When you are looking forward to something with excitement and expectation, or dreaming of the future you envision for yourself, these people rob you of your joy. They are the ones who say, "You can't do that." We want you to respond with, "Oh yes, I can. You just watch me." This is what financially successful women say when faced with naysayers. Doubting yourself never helps, as you will always have people who will do that for you.

When Ardelle was talking about buying her first condominium on her own, two colleagues who were her age and in similar income categories, but both married, told her "You can't do that." Although she didn't respond out loud, Ardelle said to herself, "Oh yes, I can. You just watch me," which was an attitude she maintained.

Ignoring the naysayers and telling yourself that you are capable affirms the positive mindset you need in order to accomplish the goals you set for yourself. It sets determination, makes you even more driven to stay positive and focused, and is what makes you walk over hot coals to make something happen. It made Ardelle work extra jobs, spend $5 on entertainment, including dates (because she found so many great activities that are cheap or free), and save every penny she could. She saw every dollar she spent as a decision and a trade-off, so she prioritized and spent mainly on what she wanted and used the most. Single, on her own, with no help from others, she surprised her colleagues and probably also a few friends and family members. And as she was walking through the door of her first condo, they were left to wonder why they didn't do it themselves. "Oh yes, I can. You just watch me," is how you take a negative influence and turn it into motivation.

Negative situations can either hold us back or give us the power to rise and succeed. There are countless examples of women who came from little, or who had to start again on their own, and have achieved financial success. Many have done it while raising children—in whose faces they found their biggest motivation to make difficult choices, work hard and save more. These women were driven to succeed not only to provide for their children but also for themselves, and to secure their own financial future. Arlene Dickinson, who is regarded as one of Canada's top female entrepreneurs and is well-known for her role on *Dragon's Den*, is very open about her personal story of being flat broke and on her own with four young kids.

Sheer grit and determination not only picked her up off the floor but took her to financial heights many can only dream of. The point is, you can overcome negative situations. With a strong will, you can turn tough circumstances into your motivation to overcome not just hurdles, but mountains.

CHOOSE YOUR SUPPORT TEAM CAREFULLY

When choosing your support team, be it the professionals you work with or the personal role models you surround yourself with, take care to choose positive influences. Who do you admire and want to be like? How did these people accomplish their goals, and how might they be able to help you achieve yours? Are the members of your team supportive? Do they care about you and your goals? Do they help build your confidence?

Remember, you are the leading lady. The people and circumstances that surround you are in supporting roles, not starring in or directing your life story. You can influence the script and your future chapters by choosing the degree to which you keep positive influences around you and turn negative influences into motivators. Just remember, it's your story—not anyone else's.

WHEN YOU HAVE THE SUPPORT OF A PARTNER

So far, our message has been largely about being self-sufficient in the journey to financial independence, because, as has been made clear, for the significant majority of women, their journey will include being single at least a portion of the time. But, for those who are presently living a partnered life, it isn't your race to run alone. Your spouse is going to play an exceptionally important role in your financial health today, and in your financial future. And so, your spouse needs to be a partner not just in life but in the journey toward your financial independence as well.

There is a delicate balancing act required when it comes to planning as a couple: recognizing that the steps you take together today will have a profound impact on your ability to become financially independent as a couple, while also recognizing the necessity for you to be fully involved in your combined financial picture and to consider your own interests should you find yourself single again. Simply because you are partnered does not mean you get a free pass. You, too, need to build your independent streak—not apart from your partner, but in concert with your partner and potentially for your single-again self.

Leslie and her husband, Michael, married at age 24, a young age by today's norms. Believe it or not, that is a year later than Michael thought they should get married. Having grown up in a one-stoplight town and attended university in a different one-stoplight town, before getting married Leslie needed to prove to herself that she could live in the big city and make it on her own—not just then, but in case she ever had to in the future. The expectation was not that she will someday be single again, she just recognized that no one knows what tomorrow will bring.

Chances are, for many women, single-again life will happen. Make sure that you've given it some thought and planned for it before it happens to you, even if you are in a great committed relationship today.

Trust—It's a Big (and Scary) Word

In any relationship, trust can actually be the biggest challenge to overcome in order to secure your potentially single-again future. We aren't talking about "trust issues" that some people have, or the trustworthiness of your partner. No, there are two other aspects of trust that can cause us problems.

The first is having blind trust and a willingness to completely abdicate financial responsibilities to someone else—this is unacceptable. You don't get a free pass, no matter how much support you have; you don't get to take the easy way out. No matter how much you trust another person, even if it's your partner or spouse, to take care of all things financial, or how little interest you have in money matters, or how much you believe in the lasting power of your relationship, you absolutely need to be involved in financial planning and management, for two very important reasons:

1. If you aren't involved at all in the finances, imagine being suddenly single again and having to start unexpectedly with no idea of where to begin, who to call or where the financial resources are—especially at a time when you are emotionally raw from losing your partner.

2. You don't know what you don't know! If you aren't involved in the finances, how on earth will you know if there is a problem your partner doesn't recognize or is too scared to tell you about? Not that you expect that, but it has happened to many others!

The second aspect about trust that can be problematic is that some women fear that wanting to be engaged in the family finances will make their significant other feel that they are not trusted! If this is a concern, you need to overcome it right away. The healthy mindset in a healthy relationship should be: "If something were to happen to me, I would want my spouse to be okay. Financially, this means not only having adequate resources, but also having the confidence and ability to manage them well." Absolutely no exceptions.

FINANCIAL SUCCESS LOOKS GOOD ON YOU

We have actually heard some single women express the fear that if they become financially successful, they will be seen as being so independent that they will be neither appealing nor available to potential life partners. Essentially, they say they feel that it would make them seem intimidating. This is nothing but an excuse not to take responsibility for themselves and their future. No woman has to fear remaining single because she has achieved financial success. There are many examples of women who created their own financial independence and it only added to their confidence—confidence that strengthened their relationships. (In Ardelle's case, over time, her financial independence started to draw a somewhat different quality of male to her and eliminate others from having a relationship with her. Thank goodness!)

There is another camp of single women who are looking to find a partner with whom to share their life but who are hoping for someone to support them financially. These women are counting on a future relationship to provide them with a nice lifestyle and financial security, instead of taking responsibility for providing this for themselves.

If you are currently single, either by choice or by circumstance, you cannot afford to sit back financially and wait. When it comes to financial independence, time matters. None of us has time to waste. One woman in our focus group shared with us that she had always thought she would marry, until one day in mid-life she woke up and realized that she probably would remain single her whole life, meaning that, financially, it was going to be all on her! Fortunately, she had always been responsible with her finances and was able to own her condo. But her big regret is that she hadn't been saving as much as she should have been and now has the big challenge of playing catch-up so she can provide for herself in the future.

Another woman, who had always planned that she would marry and be able to be home with her children, nonetheless pursued a career during her single years. She did eventually marry, but she credits her working years and her savings in addition to her husband's as being what made it possible for the two of them to buy a family home together and to afford to be a one-income household when their children were young.

There is no downside to being single and financially responsible. In fact, not only will it help you should you remain single, it will help you and your partner or family get ahead if you enter a relationship—and it might just make finding that right person easier! Let's be honest, if you are looking for someone who is financially responsible, they might just be looking for the same trait and asking themselves that very question about you. But what we don't want is for any woman to rely on finding a partner to fulfill that role. If you want your partner to be your financial out simply because of your own self-doubt or fear of not being able to do it on your own, that puts you in a very precarious position—both within the relationship as well as if you end up staying single or becoming single again.

FROM FEARFUL TO FEAR LESS

Let's be honest, we all feel fear and self-doubt at times. Some may feel these emotions more acutely than others, but these are unnerving feelings we can all relate to in one way or another. When it comes to finances, and financial decisions, fear and self-doubt can be particularly intense; they have the power either to motivate us to overcome struggles, or the power to make us freeze and bury our head in the sand, thereby holding us back.

In our interviews and focus groups with women, fear was an emotion that many had in common and talked about openly. Some women actually articulated the fear of becoming a "bag lady," ending up living in poverty either in their older years or now if their life were to change in a major way. Others didn't describe the end result of financial hardship specifically, but rather, they focused on their fears around risk. Remarkably, for some the fear was that if they took risk they would experience losses, while others were concerned they weren't taking enough risk to grow what they had into what they intrinsically knew they needed. Financially, at the heart of these fears is the same issue: the fear of not having enough to be able to sustain one's lifestyle for a lifetime.

Some people are so fearful they are frozen. The thought of negative possibilities overwhelms them. They can deal only with the present, and this actually prevents them from taking the necessary steps to protect themselves in the future. We heard this in our focus groups. Those we spoke to who were single, either again or had been for their whole life, recognized that the weight of having to accomplish financial independence is fully on their own shoulders, and this burden held some of them back. The self-doubt about being able to make it on their own prevented them from taking charge.

Fear and self-doubt can also prevent us from facing the truth and/ or making a necessary change. It is easy to allow ourselves to remain busy doing other, less important, things that use up our time and energy so that we don't have to deal with what should be our priority. Remember, timing is everything. The more time you waste putting it off simply makes the task harder.

While fear can hold us back, it can also be an incredible motivator that drives us to success. Fear motivates many people to do everything they can to loosen the bonds of financial hardship, to shake off the weight and move forward stronger and more secure. It makes them do the things they have to do, and it moves them from fearful to fearless (or, to fear less). Those who achieve a financially "fear less" state must first feel secure. Feelings of financial security come from having sufficient resources to protect ourselves. Like everything, building that takes time and effort.

To protect yourself, you must prepare yourself in case your situation was to change tomorrow—for example, a change in your employment, health or relationship status. Upheaval in any of these areas is stressful enough; add financial stress, and it makes thing worse. Your protection is having savings and knowing you have access to money when the unexpected happens. Being financially prepared gives you options and can buy you time. Simply having savings or insurance that provides income in the event of injury or disability, for example, allows you to feel more confident that, should your life change for the worse, you'll have the resources to weather the storm and protect yourself. This is security. Feelings of security allow you the freedom to take the risks you need to take to achieve a lifetime of income that provides financial independence.

An established professional shared with us that she had long feared the bag lady syndrome she had studied in a psychology course during her university years. That fear ensured that she never lived beyond her means, and it motivated her to save aggressively not only for the long term, but also just in case she lost a job, had a health issue or faced some other crisis. In her spending and her planning, she never counted on a getting a raise or having a partner. She finally realized she had gotten to the point where the likelihood of living in poverty was very slim given her age, accomplishments and the assets she had worked hard to accumulate. In fact, she had achieved financial independence. Her anxiety caused by the fear of being a bag lady was a big motivator behind her success.

Like the women we interviewed, Ardelle at a younger age most feared not having enough money to live a comfortable lifestyle and no longer being able to take care of herself financially. She was also fearful that she would become like some women she knew: financially dependent on a husband and trapped in an unhappy marriage. These possibilities drove Ardelle to be prepared in case her circumstances changed, especially regarding her health or employment. She was motivated to protect herself—to own her home, pay off her mortgage and have adequate insurance and savings set aside in case she couldn't earn income during her remaining working years. Her deepest financial fears drove her to prioritize building multiple future income sources so that she could become financially independent, retire when she wanted and remain comfortable during her retirement.

The transition from being fearful to "fear less" won't mean that you will never feel fear or self-doubt; however, it does mean that by addressing these emotions, not only will you be better able to identify them and cope with them, you will also learn to use them to your advantage to move forward and reach your goals. And remember, you don't have to face your fears alone. You can enlist the help of your support network to deal with and overcome negative emotions. Others have done so, and so can you.

If fear and self-doubt are preventing you from moving forward to being financially independent and successful, consider this: if you choose *not* to move forward and take positive steps, you most likely are choosing a future that is the very future you fear. If you are reading this book, then you at least recognize the importance of being responsible about your financial future. Together, we want to help you move forward.

Whether you are still single, partnered or single again, you cannot allow the powerful emotions of fear and self-doubt, or the negative influences of others, to prevent you from achieving your financial success. Failing to take responsibility for your own financial situation simply cannot be an option. You are the leading lady in your life's story. Your mindset and your ability to manage your emotions and turn negatives into motivations will have a tremendous impact on your ability to achieve financial independence. To overcome the practical and emotional challenges in your journey, not only do you need to foster your independent streak, you also need to build your confidence.

Chapter 3

THE POWER OF CONFIDENCE

Spend a moment thinking of people you know who exude confidence. You see it in their body language: they hold their shoulders back and stand up straight. But really, confidence is all about attitude. Not overconfidence that can turn into arrogance, but having a positive outlook on life; a feeling a person has that, regardless of what life throws at them, they will maintain a healthy attitude of "I can do it" and "Others have done [fill in the blank], and so can I." In many ways, you might say that confident people go through life with purpose—nothing is going to hold them back. That is the attitude all women can have when it comes to our finances. It may come more naturally to some of us than others, but having that kind of attitude is possible for us all. With a little work, and perhaps some support, we can all be a confident, self-assured, person when it comes to money matters, even if single.

Confidence is power. It is the power to overcome obstacles, such as negative emotions, which can hold you back. It is the power to make the impossible, or at least the improbable, possible. Confidence inspires us to take those actions we need to take to make our dreams happen. And we *can* make them happen. The sooner you acknowledge that you control your actions—and that, therefore, you are in far more control of the outcome than simply relying on luck or circumstance—the sooner you can take the actions you need to take to give yourself the confidence you require (if you don't already possess it) to actually accomplish your goals. If confidence is power and it provides the motivation to act in a way that positively impacts your outcomes, you must somehow build your confidence.

Later in the book we will talk about and provide tools that will help you get organized, be informed about your financial position and protect yourself in the event of the unexpected. We'll also discuss the importance of setting goals, having a plan, and saving to make those goals happen. These are all important, practical things that will help put you in control of your finances, which ultimately will build your confidence, and they are all things that many financial advisors recommend their clients do. But there are also some other more general tips (consisting of steps, habits and/or strategies) that you can use to help build up your confidence about money matters. That is what we are going to focus on in this chapter.

FINANCIAL CONFIDENCE BUILDERS

Tip 1: Talk About It

Our culture and society in general seem to shy away from any conversation about finances. For some reason, talking about money is viewed as a faux pas, kind of like talking about death and politics! But women are natural networkers who like to share experiences and challenges with others, especially with other women. So, we say, put that natural tendency to work and build your confidence by learning all you can about money from other women—or anyone who will talk with you about it.

In our focus groups, it was incredible how open women were to having a conversation about money; sharing the experiences they had in the journey that got them to where they are financially today, including the right choices they made and the errors they made along the way. As much as they hadn't really discussed these things in such detail before, they felt it was good to open up about their finances. So many of them wanted the opportunity to have someone be a sounding board for them. Intrinsically it seems they feel like knowledge, thus information, is missing. When information is missing and we feel like we don't know something, it can actually fuel feelings of insecurity, and this saps our confidence. Talking about money and learning from others has the opposite effect; it is one way to build your financial IQ and help overcome the feelings that hold you back.

Unfortunately, we don't learn much about money in school and it's even a taboo subject within some families. It's like we are all meant to learn about money the hard way. Unless you grew up in a family who taught the value of a dollar, the importance of savings and the necessity of not living above your means, and who openly discussed decisions that needed to be made about money; or you studied money-related topics in your post-secondary education—then you started your adulthood at a disadvantage. No wonder so many women have a confidence problem when it comes to money!

Not knowing enough about finances puts you at greater risk of making mistakes or, potentially even worse than making a mistake, allowing the fear of making a mistake to hold you back from taking advantage of your opportunities. So, how can you overcome this disadvantage? To start with, we can learn from one another. Just as we learn from our own successes and failures, we can learn from the successes and failures of others. Let's be honest, it is best if we can avoid making the same mistake someone else made! And why be shy about sharing our mistakes? Wouldn't it be great if we could save someone else the pain, suffering and losses we've lived through and worked so hard to recover from? We do have the power to help each other, and in helping someone else, you might just discover you know a lot more than you had been giving yourself credit for. Sharing money knowledge with others can build their confidence—and your own!

Who are the friends you trust? Who are those real, honest friends you can have a confidential conversation with? Who won't judge but will be supportive of you? Who are the mentors and people you admire? Talk to women who are a generation or two older than you, those who have been down this road before. It is amazing what we can learn from each other. Having a good conversation with someone whom you know and trust will make you feel like you are taking steps in the right direction, because you are! Those steps in the right direction will do so much in helping to build your confidence.

Start small. You don't have to talk about deeply personal things like how much you earn, how much you have invested or the debt you may have. In our focus groups, we didn't even touch on the specific details of those topics. Rather, the women discussed things like what they wished their younger self had known about money. They talked about the fear of taking risks, but also feeling like they need to take more risks at the right time. Together we talked about the good and bad experiences we all had had with things like tenants and investments. We talked about different strategies for saving and, for those women who were in relationships, different ways to handle money as a couple.

Talking to others about money doesn't have to mean sharing your financial statements with your friends and mentors. Simply speaking about financial topics will open your eyes to different ways of thinking, which could help identify a strategy that might work for you. It will also make you feel better for having learned something new, and it may make you realize that you know more than you thought!

Especially if you are single, take it to the next level and have a financial discussion with others with whom you can share your goals. Find someone you can be very open with about personal aspects of your finances and who would celebrate your successes with you. Maybe that person will also help hold you accountable in the decisions you make and challenge you to make the right decisions for yourself toward accomplishing what matters most to you. Maybe she is a great friend, family member or mentor. As will be discussed in Chapter 13, the right professional advisor can help fill that role in your life.

Talking about your finances, learning from others and realizing you know more than you think you do, will go a long way to building lasting confidence. You just have to begin the conversation. In Chapter 14, you will find discussion questions to help you get started. For now, consider the following.

Talk About It—With Others

1. List three people you trust and would like to have a financial conversation with:

    i. _____

    ii. _____

    iii. _____

2. List some topics you would like to discuss or know more about:

    i. _____

    ii. _____

    iii. _____

Tip 2: Take a Look at Yourself

Although having a conversation about finances with others can help build confidence, perhaps even more important is the conversation we have with ourselves. What you say to yourself matters—it matters greatly. What you tell yourself about yourself shapes your confidence. If you have a positive frame of mind, you will most likely have a better outcome. Mindset matters, and only you can program your mindset.

Just as in any other aspect of your life, positive self-talk can boost your confidence about money. We don't mean you should delude yourself about your financial IQ or your financial situation; rather, you need to be able to look yourself in the mirror, which means being honest with yourself about where you stand, while building the right attitude to money matters. Facing your financial realities will help you feel more in control, and that will build your confidence, empowering you to improve your situation.

Put yourself in the position of being able to say the following to yourself: "I know where I stand financially. I know the balance of my bank account. I know I am carrying some credit card debt, but I have a plan to pay it off. The mortgage is on the way to being burned. I am going to retire early and in style." Then, whether it is the first $1,000 you have just saved, or your savings have crossed the $1 million or $2 million mark—celebrate your success. Celebrate being able to take that amazing trip without going into debt. Celebrate that you can afford to retire when expected—or maybe even earlier! Tell yourself you are going to do it and that you can do it. When you do it, or when a milestone along the way toward that goal happens, whatever the success is and no matter how small it is, celebrate it. Accomplishing and celebrating the small things will help you to keep going, ultimately helping you achieve your bigger, long-term goals. This conversation with yourself and the positive reinforcement of the reward will help you build confidence. Tell yourself: You are a financial success! To help you get the conversation with yourself going, complete the following questions.

Talk About It—With Yourself

1. List some of the money messages you tell yourself:

   i. _____

   ii. _____

2. What financial information or realities do you need to face to know where you stand and to improve your financial situation going forward?

3. What are some of the positive messages you will tell yourself about money and your financial goals going forward?

Tip 3: Ask Yourself, What's Your Motto?

Having a motto can inspire you to act and to overcome challenges. It can help you stay focused and make decisions as you work toward your goals; and, very importantly, whatever stands in your way, a motto can give you the motivation to overcome it. A motto gives you purpose.

A good financial motto boils down to those things that bring you joy, the things you value most. Those things for which you would happily sacrifice something nice or fun today (let's say, a manicure) to have the opportunity to do something that matched those values in the long run (maybe going on the trip of a lifetime, owning your own home or making a career change). You would be willing and motivated to sacrifice that manicure today to be able to save those dollars toward that trip, a home or whatever it is you value most, because you would get more value, more joy from it than you would a manicure. The right financial motto for you reflects the things that you will always value most, regardless of where life takes you.

Create a financial motto that empowers you, motivates you and helps you prioritize. Keep it short—just a few words or one brief sentence—to reflect only the goals and qualities that are most important to you. It can help keep you on track financially and focused on what truly matters. And it can actually help you make decisions. Imagine someone with a motto of "Family and Friends, Adventure and Charity." You can imagine that this person probably has a fairly active lifestyle. Her relationships are very important to her and, therefore, she probably enjoys spending time with those special people. She is also very charitably minded. Most likely, giving financially to a variety of causes, and potentially giving her time to help others as well, is a priority for her. A motto can be a very powerful tool, but very few people actually have one. Developing a motto is a simple investment that costs you nothing. It can pay you back many times over by acting as a guiding principle in your life, which will help provide clarity around financial choices and enhance your confidence in the decisions you make.

Take some time to create your own motto. Start by simply making a list of words that are specific to your values, like family or friends;

you can also choose terms that are broader, like laughter, fun or adventure. The point is, they are things that really won't change in terms of how you value them. Your life may change and maybe one element of your motto might evolve to some extent, but generally it is a rare event that would have you change your motto. It is a reflection of your true self, your core values. It is authentic. And having a motto will help you make financial decisions with confidence, knowing they are the right ones for you.

What's Your Motto?

1. What are the qualities that resonate with you? What are the words that capture the essence of those things in life that bring you joy? List them.

Ideas to get you started:

Family	Fun	Work/Career
Friends	Charity	Success
Laughter	Faith	Health
Adventure	Knowledge	Fitness

What are the words that resonate with you (not just from the list above)? What are your words?

i. _____

ii. _____

iii. _____

iv. _____

2. Putting it together, what is your motto, slogan or guideline?

_____

_____

Tip 4: Ask Yourself, What Is Your Vision for Your Future?

If you were to write the story of your life, how would you want it to read? Your motto is a guiding force, but your vision is based on much more: the people and the relationships that matter most to you; the things and the activities that bring you joy. What are your interests? What are your goals? Imagine you achieve these goals, how would it feel? Who do you want beside you as you go through life? These elements are, in essence, the heart of your vision. The things that make a rich, full life don't necessarily all include money; however, anything that makes your life rich that requires money also requires planning to make it possible.

It is amazing how working toward a goal that is part of your vision can create confidence. So often, people simply save blindly. We know we are supposed to save, we hear it all the time—from parents who encouraged us to save from a young age, in advertisements from banks, in articles in the newspaper and so on. Often, we simply save because it is something the world tells us to do. We have no idea if we are saving enough or if we are saving too much. And really, what are we saving for? The reason you save should be to help you achieve your vision.

Perhaps you want to travel extensively. If so, save with that intention; save with the purpose of travel in mind. Perhaps you want to achieve financial independence (we certainly want this for you!). What does financial independence look like to you? What does it feel like? Saving toward things that you can envision is a whole lot easier than simply saving blindly. If you can imagine what financial independence looks like and feels like to you, then you will be far more willing and able to make the sacrifices that are necessary for you to put money aside. And guess what? When you save with intention, toward your plan, it builds confidence that you are doing what you need to do to achieve your vision. When you are making it happen, when you see the progress you are making, it builds even more confidence.

Financial confidence isn't something that you just wake up one morning and suddenly have. It takes effort and time to build. Regardless of where you are starting today, you can take steps to make yourself stronger.

Seven Questions to Help You Clarify Your Vision

1. Who are the important people in your life?

2. What would you like to do with/for these people?

3. What are your interests?

4. If you could be doing anything right now, what would it be? Where would you be? Who would you be with?

5. How happy are you with your career? Would you change anything about it?

6. When you retire, how do you want to spend your time?

7. When you look back on your life, what would you be most proud of having accomplished?

A marathon runner, before being ready to run a full marathon, first has to be able to run one mile, then two miles and five miles before being able to accomplish the goal of completing 26.2 miles. It takes time to build the muscles, the stamina and the mindset to make it possible. And so, too, it takes time to build confidence. But talking with others, talking positively to yourself, creating a motto that reflects who you really are and clarifying your vision for your future will go a long way to helping you build yourself up.

These are not mutually exclusive tools. In fact, talking about money needs to happen over time. Regardless of your age, as you go through life it will be important to talk to others you respect about financial issues, to debate strategies and to always think and speak positively about yourself and your financial future. Even in darker times, look forward with optimism. Don't let a mistake or setback hold you back. Learn something from it and move on. In fact, it is important to give yourself permission to make a mistake—we all make them. How you deal with a mistake and overcome it can actually help build confidence! When you look back, you'll see that simply having survived, persevered and come out the other side made you stronger.

Your motto and your vision are uniquely intertwined. In fact, something is wrong if the elements of your vision don't match your motto. If something isn't aligned, you need to ask yourself, is that really part of your vision? Or is something missing from your motto? There are no right or wrong ways to articulate your motto or your vision. But they do need to reflect each other. Ultimately, they both need to be a reflection of your true, authentic self. They need to represent the things in life that are most important to you; to help you focus on the things that you would walk over hot coals to achieve. They are things that motivate you, the events and goals that you can picture—and you can visualize the emotions you will feel when you are successful.

When you have a financial decision to make, look at your motto and your vision and ask yourself: "If I do this, will it help me achieve my vision, or is it going to hurt my ability to achieve what really matters?" Through that lens, you can have confidence in making good decisions—choices that you will look back on and be glad you made. Referring to the priorities your motto and vision are based on will give you confidence to move forward, or make you feel better about saying no.

Confidence matters. Confidence is power. Building your financial confidence will ultimately lead to you being able to achieve your vision and enjoy financial independence.

Chapter **4**

BE INFORMED
Raise Your Financial IQ

You don't know what you don't know. And when it comes to finances, ignorance really is *not* bliss. In fact, whether or not you are single, realizing that you may not fully know your financial situation, or whether or not you are on track to achieving your goals, can in and of itself result in fear and, ultimately, insecurity. We want you to feel confident about your financial position. Although it may feel harder having to do it all on your own, one of the best steps you can take to feel in control of your current situation as well as your financial future is to bring all the pieces of your financial puzzle together on one page, so you can have everything in one place and see the big picture. In fact, this goes for anyone, regardless of whether you are single or partnered. Being informed about your finances gives you confidence to make important decisions that are aligned with your goals not only today, but also with your goals for the future.

Many of our focus group participants expressed how a lack of knowledge about investing has held them back. This feeling of being ill-informed has made them fearful of taking the risk that they actually recognize they need to take. And investing is only one financial area that intimidates or unnerves people. Estate planning, for example, is a subject that many people simply don't want to know anything about because they don't want to contemplate their own death, never mind plan for it. But when it comes to your finances, not being informed isn't the solution.

Debt is another difficult reality to face, but it is a financial fact of life for most people, given that you usually need to take on debt to buy a home, a car or a vacation property, or to fund your post-secondary education. Debt can be a powerful tool to help you achieve your goals. But debt is also so powerful that, if it's used incorrectly or you have too much of it, it can seriously derail your plans or, worse, push you into financial crisis. Being informed about debt is important, especially for the single woman, not just to make sure you don't get in over your head, but also as an opportunity to help build wealth.

We talked about the importance of financial confidence in Chapter 3. Critical to having such confidence is having knowledge. Being informed about your overall financial situation, about your assets (including savings and investments) and your debt, puts you in control and makes for a financially confident, and competent, woman. This may sound daunting, but trust us, it shouldn't be. There are some simple things that can help build your knowledge and give you confidence in making investment and financial planning choices. In fact, we will show you how little time it actually takes to be informed.

BRINGING IT ALL TOGETHER

Regardless of your age, life stage or marital status, this first step of bringing it all together is extremely important. To begin with, you may just be surprised by what you find. Some people experience shock at how much wealth they actually have accumulated when they bring it all together. In fact, through working on her clients' financial plans, Leslie has been the one to point out to a number of people that they have over a million in investments. Why didn't they know this? Because their financial lives had been scattered between work and personal savings plans here, there and everywhere, and they just hadn't put it all together to be able to see what they had achieved. They are millionaires, and they didn't even know it! It is more common than you think.

We can all agree that finding out you are a millionaire and didn't know it is a pleasant surprise. However, when some people bring all their financial information together, they might just find out the opposite—that there is a problem. If you find out you have a problem, burying your head in the sand isn't the answer. Even having more money won't necessarily solve your financial problems if managing and organizing money is an issue for you. Solving money problems takes a willingness to assess the situation, make plans for the future and make any necessary changes so that you'll be able to accomplish your objectives.

If, upon looking at your full financial picture, you do find out you have a problem, with either saving or spending, for example, this is your opportunity to intervene—to take control of your situation and take the steps to improve it, regardless of how long doing so might take. Remember, your older self is relying on your younger self to make the right plans and choices for the long term. The sooner you find out you have a problem, the faster you can fix it by taking action and making the necessary changes. Ignoring the issue will just make it worse, causing the hole to get bigger and become harder to dig out of. In fact, not sorting it out may leave you with fewer choices in the future. Not only does not informing yourself and not intervening on your own behalf put your ability to achieve financial independence in doubt, you may be at risk of not even achieving financial security!

Another reason for bringing it all together is that having the full financial picture from the outset provides a starting point for tracking your progress through time. You can see your mortgage or other liabilities decline as you pay them off; you can see your savings grow over time; and if there are any hiccups, you can adjust accordingly to get back on track. Seeing your progress over time helps build your confidence—you are doing it, it is working. And we all know we should do more of what is working for us, and less of what isn't.

Finally, when you bring all the pieces of your financial puzzle together, it brings you peace of mind because you are in control. You know where everything is; nothing hidden, so there is no fear of the unknown. It sounds simple. It is simple: being informed brings confidence. The best part is, it actually doesn't take a lot of time. (Later in this chapter we will walk you through how to do your personal financial inventory.)

THE INFORMED SINGLE WOMAN

If you are single, whether by design or by circumstance, it is all on you—the finances are solely on your shoulders. This brings challenges: one income, one pension (if you have one) and one set of government benefits in your senior years. It also brings opportunities: you get to make all the decisions, and if you choose to take a risk, it impacts you only (assuming you do not have any dependents). Being informed about your finances is an absolute necessity because there's no one else to take charge. Achieving financial independence won't happen if you don't take control and assume responsibility for it. Great things happen by intention; they don't just fall into your lap.

There are too many women who barely get by in their later years. Many must continue working at an age when they shouldn't have to. Sometimes this is due to unfortunate circumstance, but for others, it is because they didn't plan ahead. They chose to live day by day, didn't take their financial inventory, and didn't save and build assets or create wealth that they could turn into income later. In short, they didn't take responsibility for themselves, and now their older self isn't very happy with their younger self.

There are legal secretaries who retire wealthy, while the lawyers they worked for enjoy their designer handbags, suits and penthouses but will have to work much longer because they spent everything rather than saving some of their working wealth. The legal secretary has made her financial inventory and built upon it; the lawyer didn't make the effort. The lawyer has the opportunity to build exceptional wealth through her working years, but by not being informed about her financial position beyond knowing her income, it meant she didn't know when to say no, financially. As we've said already, you don't know what you don't know. One woman (the legal secretary) will enjoy a comfortable retirement, while the other woman (the lawyer) may have to work during her retirement and take a big step down in lifestyle.

Leslie has learned in her advisory practice never to underestimate the ability of a lower-income employee to build more wealth than her boss. She has also seen how two people with the same income can have tremendously different outcomes: One legal secretary made the effort to be informed and now reaps the rewards. Another doesn't make the effort and can't ever enjoy financial independence. One lawyer has to work in retirement, while another lawyer with the same income built tremendous wealth, ensuring not only financial independence but also the freedom to do what she had once only dreamed of doing. Without fail, the defining difference is that one was informed about her financial position, and the other wasn't.

One of the big excuses single people make about why they can't take financial inventory and be informed is that they are "doing it on their own and are bad at math" and don't like working with numbers or spreadsheets. This is a cop out. Simple addition and subtraction are all that are needed. If you want, you can even use a calculator! If that is too much for you, there are simple computer programs that do the work for you. On the *Plan Single* website, (www.plansingle.ca) you will find a tool that will do the hard work for you. Regardless if math is not your strength or interest, you can still manage your financial position so that you don't set yourself up for disaster.

A recently divorced woman came out of her breakup with significant assets and support payments. Because she thinks she is "bad at math," she hasn't bothered to sit down and understand what her financial resources are. She is still spending as she did when she was married. Unfortunately, she never made the effort to put in perspective to what extent her post-divorce income and assets could sustain her pre-divorce lifestyle. The sad reality is that—as much as she is receiving significant support payments and is considered very wealthy post-divorce—this is the sort of person who runs a high risk of running out of money. That's not to say she can't afford a nice lifestyle, but to spend without knowing when to say no is setting herself up for disaster. There isn't anyone else in that household to earn an income, to save or to build wealth.

If you are single, it is solely on you. The first step to achieving financial independence is knowing where you are today; not what has transpired in the past, but where you are today. Yesterday is yesterday. We can't change that. What we can do is look forward. It starts with your financial inventory.

COUPLES: EXPECT BLISS, BUT WHAT IF . . . ?

For couples, it's different. Financially you potentially have the joy of two incomes as well as two sets of pensions, work benefits and government benefits. If those assets are managed properly, your opportunities increase. If managed improperly, the risks are greater. In any relationship, there are the things one partner does, there are things the other partner does and, as we manage our busy lives, we are happy to let the other person drive the bus in certain areas of life and go along for the ride. But if you let your partner drive the financial bus and you don't at least make an effort to share in the responsibility of navigation, you are putting yourself at great risk, especially because of the likelihood of one day being single again.

It is healthy to expect bliss in your relationship; most couples will plan that their future includes each other, and this is arguably how it should be. However, it is also important to remember that 90 percent of women end up having to manage their own finances later in life, even if they are married or in a committed relationship at some point. If so many women end up single, then chances are you will be one of them. So, as much as you plan for relationship bliss and a long life together, it is smart to, at a minimum, ensure you are financially informed . . . just in case.

Let's talk about Abi and Tom, a lovely, happily married couple in their late fifties. From very early on in their relationship, retirement mattered to them. They were both willing to work hard while also enjoying life today, but they really wanted to plan for life after work. Over the years, the vast majority of major decisions in their household have been with the view to their retirement, and they have made those decisions together. Tom is interested in all things financial. Abi, not so much. However, even though Abi has happily allowed Tom to be the main manager of the finances in their home, she is involved. She is part of all the discussions and the decisions. Abi attends the meetings with their family's financial advisor. She knows about all the family assets and liabilities and where all the financial information is. She knows that their family is on track to achieving their financial goals. And, most importantly, if something were to happen to Tom, Abi won't have to deal with money worries on top of the emotional strain that would bring. Instead, she would be able to step competently into the role of making financial decisions on her own.

Bills? What Bills?

Being fully informed about your finances is not just about identifying and tracking the value of all your assets and liabilities, it also means being informed about regular bills such as property taxes and utilities. Often in a partnership, one person may take responsibility for setting up services and paying for them. If you have a partner who has this responsibility and you suddenly had to take over, would you know which companies to contact and how to gain access to the accounts, even if your partner paid the bills online and all that information is password protected?

In the age of strict privacy legislation, you need to be listed either as a joint account holder or, at minimum, as an authorized person on an account to be able to even speak to someone about it. A widow shared her experience with us. Her husband had been sent all their bills electronically, which he paid as they arrived rather than setting up automatic withdrawals. It wasn't until after his passing, when she received a notice of pending disconnection, that she realized the power bill, and probably other bills, were no longer being paid.

But what would it be like if Tom drove the financial bus and didn't share even the most basic information with Abi? Or what if Abi were so disinterested in money matters that she was to just let Tom manage everything and make all the decisions? Unfortunately, these are both scenarios that occur with some frequency. What happens if Tom were to unexpectedly pass away and Abi had not been informed about the family finances? Not only would Abi be grieving, but she would have to get a handle on the family finances! Where are the accounts? What insurance was in place? Who are the contacts for banking and accounting? How are bills paid? And where are their wills, anyway? These are just some of the issues that must be resolved very quickly, and potentially at a time of great emotional distress.

What if your spouse simply will not share financial information with you? Although it is more ideal in a committed relationship for the two of you to plan together, if that isn't an option, plan for yourself! Work with your own advisor. Set the goal that if something should happen and you become single again, you will be okay financially. Have assets that are in your own name, that you control and that only you have access to. Because if you have your own assets, you will have choice, some protection and some measure of financial security.

To protect yourself, you cannot simply abdicate the responsibility of managing the finances to your spouse. Regardless of the stage of life you are at or how blissful your relationship is, each of you must be informed about the family's full financial position. One may take care of the details, but both need to be involved in setting the goals and making decisions. You should at least know what the whole picture looks like, even if you're not the one fitting all the pieces of the puzzle together. Have regular financial check-ins: Where are you at with the mortgage? Where are you at with your savings toward your goals? Are you on track or not? Do you need to make any adjustments to your spending or to your long-term planning?

A survey conducted by the Bank of Montreal and reported by *Global News* in February 2014, found that 68 percent of participants listed fighting over money as their top reason for divorce.[7] So, being completely informed about and involved in the family finances may not be just great financial advice, it might just be great relationship advice as well!

SINGLE AGAIN

In December 2013, the Vanier Institute of the Family reported that an estimated 41 percent of marriages in Canada will end before their thirtieth wedding anniversary.[8] In addition to the high rate of divorce, an untold number of common-law relationships break down every year. According to Canadian census data from 2011, the average age at which women are widowed is fifty-six. There are many ways for women to become single again, making this an important topic to consider from a financial perspective, even if you are currently in a great relationship.

Finding yourself suddenly single again is an extremely challenging time emotionally. Your life has just radically changed. Financially, when a woman finds herself single again, it is very important to take stock. Where are you at now? What are the immediate issues that you face? The degree to which you were engaged in the finances before the event that made you single again is going to have a dramatic impact on your ability to manage your finances now and on your confidence level when it comes to money matters.

Even if you had done a financial inventory when you were part of a couple, it's essential that you repeat that exercise for your new single self because things will have changed. It is reasonable to expect that it will take some time before you are ready to move from simply paying the bills and "managing" to creating your personal financial inventory and doing your own financial planning. But don't put off that step indefinitely. It will be very important for you to take stock—take financial inventory—as soon as possible. Realistically, your plans for your future have changed, you may just not know what they have changed to yet. It will take time to see your vision for a future on your own, a vision upon which you can build a longer-term plan. But all of that starts with taking inventory, with being informed about what your new financial picture looks like. Knowing where you stand today will help you make the right decisions for you and your future.

TAKING INVENTORY

Regardless of your marital status, being informed can be as simple as completing Table 4.1 on page 45 to create your own personal financial inventory. First, list your liquid assets, the money you can access fairly quickly if you needed to. This includes not just your bank accounts but your investment accounts too, as well as longer-term savings, like your retirement accounts. Aside from specifying the value of each account, you should also identify how they can they be accessed and by whom. Who owns the account? If you are single, it is obvious—it is yours. If you are part of a couple, is it his, is it hers or is it joint?

This isn't a what's-mine-is-mine sort of thing; this ownership information is more for planning what-if scenarios. For example, do you have a tax-efficient split of assets? If everything is taxed (or is going to be taxed) in one spouse's name, there may be an opportunity for tax planning that can save you a lot of money down the road. Or, if everything is in one spouse's name, in the event of tragedy, can the surviving spouse access money quickly? If nothing is in the surviving spouse's name, what will the time delay be for him or her to actually access funds? You should also include the name of the institution that holds each account, as well as the appropriate contact person and their contact information. This information may all sound so obvious, but none of it is if you are suddenly single and don't know where to begin or who to deal with.

Next, list your fixed assets. These are things you own that may take a little time to sell, or assets that you wouldn't necessarily want to sell. This includes your home, cottage or other vacation property. Maybe you have art work, valuable jewellery or a boat. Potentially your car. Only list the most valuable assets, and their approximate value. After you've finished listing your fixed assets, list your liabilities: your debts, such as a mortgage, car loan, student debt, lines of credit and so on. What is the outstanding balance of each?

If we add up your assets and subtract your liabilities, voilà! We have your net worth. Ideally, every year that net worth, the difference between what you own and what you owe, should increase. That's essentially what taking your financial inventory is about: understanding what you own and what you owe, and having that information at hand so you can see easily if you are making progress. It helps you make decisions about paying down debt or saving more; it helps you simply be informed and have confidence, giving you peace of mind that it is all under control.

Want to be informed and stay informed? It can be as simple as doing the following:

- Once a year, sit down and update the values on your financial inventory tracking sheet (review and complete it together if you are part of a couple). Calculate your new net worth. (Time needed: 30 minutes.)

- Have a meeting with your advisor to review your inventory, as well as your progress toward your big goals. (Time needed: 1.5 hours.)

TABLE 4.1: Your Financial Inventory

Type/Name	Institution Name	Account/Policy Number	Owner	Value	Contact Person
Description	Company Where Held	ABC12345	(Individual or Joint)	Current Value	Name & Number
Liquid Assets (Chequing, Savings, RRSP, TFSA, Defined Contribution Pension, etc.)					
1					
2					
3					
4					
5					
6					
			Total Liquid Assets	**$**	
Fixed Assets (Real Estate; Owned Cars, Boats, Art, Valuable collectibles, etc.)					
1					
2					
3					
4					
5					
			Total Liquid Assets	**$**	
			TOTAL ASSETS (liquid + fixed)	**$**	
Liabilities (Mortgages, Car Loans, Student Debt, Credit Card Debt, etc.)					
1					
2					
3					
4					
5					
			Total Liabilities	**$**	
		YOUR NET WORTH (total assets - liabilities)		**$**	

Ideally, your net worth increases each year

There you have it. Put in a total of two hours a year, and you can actually be reasonably informed. And yet it is amazing: so many people won't spend two hours a year on something as incredibly important as their whole financial future, yet they will spend hours planning a week-long vacation. Whether or not you take an active role in monitoring your financial situation and planning your financial future may make the difference between being able to travel in later years or not, and between attaining or not attaining any of the long-term goals you set for yourself.

Taking financial inventory is something *you* have to do. No one else can do it for you. You (and a spouse if you are married) are the only one(s) who can pull this information together. So, take the time now to fill out Table 4.1.

The great thing about this tracking sheet is that once you have your information inputted, very little actually changes; the major entries can stay the same for years or even decades. In fact, many times it will just be the value of your assets and outstanding debts that change. Spend one hour on initially setting it up, and it can work for you for years.

BE INFORMED ABOUT INVESTMENTS

So far, we have talked about the importance of being informed from a big-picture perspective. There's no question, understanding your assets is an important part of being informed about your financial picture. Bank accounts are pretty self-explanatory, and we will talk about real estate in Chapter 12. However, to really leverage the power of your money, it is important to be informed about investment and debt; to know how to mitigate your risks and put them to work for you. But the one area where there is a lot of uncertainty tends to be with investments.

When it comes to managing investments, you can do it yourself or you can work with an advisor. If you have the knowledge, the skill and the inclination to invest yourself, fantastic. Detailed how-to investing is beyond the scope of this book, but there are plenty of resources out there to help you do that simply and cost effectively.

But be aware that investing can be complicated. If you don't feel you have the knowledge, the skill or the inclination to manage it yourself, you can work with a professional advisor. In fact, it is probably the prudent thing to do in that circumstance.

But just because you "outsource" managing your investments to a professional advisor, it doesn't mean you are handing over the responsibility and shouldn't ask questions (and there are no dumb questions); you need to be engaged in the process to some degree because nobody cares about your money as much as you do. Even if you choose to work with an advisor, take the time to review your statements, meet with your advisor and ensure your account is being managed according to your goals. These steps are all part of being informed. You don't have to make the day-to-day investment decisions or become a do-it-yourself investor, but taking these simple steps will build your knowledge over time and give you peace of mind that you are on the right track.

In our focus group discussions, the topic of risk came up often. In fact, many women expressed that they are scared to take risk because they don't feel informed about investments in general, or because they don't have complete confidence in their investment strategies. Regardless of the reasons, the end result is the same: their savings aren't growing as much as they need to, which is holding them back from achieving their financial goals.

If you are like these women, you actually have a thirst for knowledge and just don't know where to find the information you need. If this is the case, start reading the financial news once a week. Maybe Saturday mornings while you're enjoying your cup of coffee. Financial news means not just whether the stock market was up or down last week (the market is a fickle thing, and following the short-term ups and downs will drive you mad!), and it's certainly not the three quick-pick stocks some trader thinks will shoot out the lights next week. No, we are talking about the real financial news—about the economy, about trends in industry, about earnings of different companies. Over time, this will help improve your knowledge. From here, if you are interested, you can read books about how to invest, or even take some continuing education courses if you feel so inclined.

All of these things will help build your financial IQ. For many, simply reading the financial section in newspapers, cruising financial websites and listening to the financial news is enough to be informed and build confidence.

If you are presently investing on your own or with limited advice, it may be time to start looking for a professional advisor. Perhaps you simply need someone to explain things to you and help guide you. Or, if you are already working with an advisor and you aren't comfortable with the recommendations she is making, or if you feel like she is talking a different language than you speak, that advisor may not be the right one for you. Feeling better informed may be as simple as looking for a new advisor. One who speaks your language, who understands your needs and goals and who recommends investments specifically to help you reach your long-term objectives. When investment decisions are presented in that context, it can help ease your mind about investing in general and about taking the appropriate amount of risk.

Being informed about your specific investments or your broader investment strategy, just like understanding your current overall financial situation, is a confidence booster. They are vital elements in putting you on the path to achieving financial independence. And remember, financial independence means being able to spend time doing the things that bring you joy.

BE INFORMED ABOUT DEBT

Debt is a potent financial concept that can have an enormous effect on your financial health. If used properly, it has the power to propel you forward; and it also has the power to derail your best-laid plans. You may have heard people reference "good" debt and "bad" debt, and there are a variety of different definitions about what good debt is and what bad debt is. But first of all, let's be clear: debt means you owe money. And someday, you have to pay that money back.

Debt is a far more common, and a far bigger, problem in our society than you may realize. In September 2017, Statistics Canada reported that, for every dollar of disposable income, on average

Canadians owe $1.71.[9] Now, of course, there are times in life when high debt-to-income levels are a reality—for instance, students with high debt but low income. Or when people are in their high-expense years with new mortgages and perhaps children in daycare. But the most worrisome statistic is that seniors are the group with the fastest-growing level of debt—arguably the one demographic that can least afford to carry debt and pay it down.[10] No matter what stage of life you are in, if you are carrying debt, be sure to have a plan to pay it off in a reasonable time frame, and certainly before you retire. If you're single, making a dent in your debt can be even more challenging because you have just one income to work with—all the more reason for you to pay attention to this issue and be informed about it.

In our view, good debt is anything that helps you build wealth, provided the level of debt isn't going to break you or cause you so much stress trying to carry it that it harms you. It's debt that is manageable. The type of debt that, if life throws you a curve ball (as has been known to happen), you have a plan that can still handle carrying that debt. For instance, if a student needs to use debt to put herself through school, that can be considered good debt, provided she has a plan for how to turn that education into income that will, in turn, pay off that debt and provide a launching pad for building future wealth.

A mortgage is the ultimate in using debt to build wealth. If used wisely, it's an example of good, smart debt. You are using the bank's money to build your own personal wealth. When you first take out a mortgage, you may really own only 20 percent of that house or condo, and the bank owns 80 percent. But as the value of your property increases, 100 percent of that increase is yours! You initially owned only 20 percent of that asset, but you get 100 percent of the upside minus the cost of the mortgage.

Let's say you bought a place for $500,000. You put down $100,000 and the bank lent you the remaining $400,000. Over time, if your property goes up 20 percent in value to $600,000, that $100,000 increase is all yours. It isn't just a 20-percent increase for you, it is actually a 100-percent increase on your initial investment! Your equity (your share of the value of the house after you have paid off the mortgage) has gone from $100,000 to $200,000, and this doesn't include the amount of debt you have paid down by making regular mortgage payments. That is the ultimate in using debt to build wealth. Again, this only really works if you can comfortably afford those mortgage payments.

Another example of using debt to build wealth is borrowing to invest. It works the same as borrowing to buy a house, but instead of the asset being a home, it's a good-quality investment portfolio. The difference being, if the investment portfolio is structured to produce an income, that income can be used to pay the interest on the debt. For instance, you borrow $500,000 to invest. The dividend income from the portfolio pays the interest, and the capital grows at 6 percent per year. In ten years, that $500,000 has grown to nearly $900,000. Now, you will have to pay some tax on that $400,000 gain, but the point is, you have just used the bank's money to build your own wealth and get you closer to your goal of financial independence. The portfolio itself has paid at least a portion of the interest. This is similar to having a tenant help pay your mortgage. Only, this way, you don't have to be a landlady!

Borrowing to invest can be smart debt, provided you can manage it, are comfortable with the risk and have a long-term view. Unlike real estate that you can touch and feel, investments aren't tangible. Real estate is valued only when it is transacted, so you don't see the daily changes in value. With market-linked investments, their value changes not each business day but each minute, and you can follow the ups and downs online or see them monthly when your statements arrive. No one minds the ups, but with ups also come periods of down. You need to be comfortable not just with the investment strategy you are following, you also need to be able to weather the downs and avoid situations where you are forced to sell at a bad time.

Taking on any kind of debt must be considered very carefully. Even good debt used with the expectation of building wealth can easily turn into bad debt if markets change or if your circumstances change and you find yourself overextended. Remember, when interest rates go up, so does the cost of your debt. By historical standards, at the time of printing we are at exceptionally low rates of interest. What may seem to be manageable debt levels today can quickly become unmanageable tomorrow if rates rise. If this can happen even with good debt (think of it as too much of a good thing), we better be extra careful about bad debt.

Whereas good debt can help to propel you forward to achieving your vision for your future, bad debt can crush you financially in potentially damaging and irreparable ways. If you are going to use debt as a tool, it's important to have a healthy respect for it and a sound strategy to manage it. Remember, debt is something you do have to pay back—and not only do you have to pay it back, you have to pay it back with interest. So, if you are spending beyond your means and carrying a lot of debt, or borrowing at high interest rates, that debt may be making your financial situation much worse rather than helping you to achieve your goals. In fact, carrying too much debt is one sure route to financial crisis.

The Real Cost of Credit Card Debt

Making only minimum payments on a credit card is like cycling on a stationary bike: you are doing something, but you never move forward and get anywhere. Using the online Credit Card Payment Calculator provided by the Financial Consumer Agency of Canada, you may be shocked to realize that an outstanding balance of $5,000 charged at an 18-percent annual interest rate would take thirteen years and ten months to pay off if all you paid was the minimum payments (3 percent per month, or $25— whichever amount is greater). Assuming you charged nothing else to your card during that time, not only would it take you almost fourteen years to pay off your balance, but you would pay almost $4,500 in interest, which is almost the full amount of your purchases.

If you have a debt that is backed by an asset—such as a house, a car or an investment portfolio—the interest rate is going to be lower and cost you less than if the debt isn't backed by an asset. The higher the interest rate, the more money you will have to pay on top of the amount you originally borrowed. Credit cards, for example, charge exorbitant interest. A credit card should be used for convenience only and paid off each and every month. If you pay it off in full each month, you don't pay any interest. But if you don't pay it off, you will be charged an annual interest rate of 10 to 20 percent, or even more!

Avoid carrying credit card debt, at all costs—it is the equivalent of an albatross around your neck. High-interest credit card debt is the epitome of bad debt. Many times, bad debt results from spending money you don't have on consumer goods and services—in other words, living beyond your means. Basically, overspending is funding a lifestyle that is unsustainable on your income alone. Again—and we can't stress it enough—this is bad debt, and it must be avoided at all costs. Remember, your older self is relying on your younger self to be financially responsible, regardless of your age.

Being informed about your current financial situation will identify any challenges you may have with debt, or it may open the door to opportunities to use debt to your advantage, but you have to be informed about it. With any debt there are risks and, as with any financial strategy you use, you need to understand what those risks are. If life throws you a curve ball, you need to be able to carry your debt, or else you will have to sell assets to cover it. Very importantly, if a bank says no to lending you money, you really should heed their warning (barring some unusual circumstance). The moment you have to go to a secondary lender whose lending standards aren't so stringent, it should be a wake-up call that you might have a problem or might be getting yourself into deep financial trouble. You could end up paying high interest rates and potentially be unable to afford that debt. The last thing you want to be is a slave to your debt, whether that be student loans, credit cards, lines of credit, car payments or mortgage payments. Many people have gotten themselves into that situation and it's very hard, sometimes impossible, to get out of the hole once you are deep in debt.

INFORMATION: YOUR LAUNCHING PAD TO FINANCIAL INDEPENDENCE

Being informed is not only about building confidence, but also about setting the stage to help you achieve financial independence. Being informed means knowing where you presently stand financially. It means understanding and being comfortable with your investment strategy, as well as being in a comfortable spot with debt. If any of these three things are off, you won't feel as confident as you should, it will hold you back from making decisions for your future and it will present a roadblock to achieving the dream—financial independence.

Here is a summary of the steps you can follow to become financially informed:

- Take your financial inventory—create your statement of net worth. (More tools are available on www.plansingle.ca.)

- If you aren't feeling informed about investing, read the financial news. You will be surprised at just how much this will increase your knowledge significantly over time.

- Is your investment strategy geared toward helping you achieve your goals? Aligning an investment strategy specifically to your goals goes a long way in helping you take the right amount of risk—risk you are comfortable with and that will get you to where you want to be.

- Evaluate whether or not you need a wealth advisor (a.k.a. financial advisor) or if you should change advisors—make sure she speaks in language you can understand and she is working on your behalf to help you achieve your goals.

- Evaluate your debt—is it good debt or bad debt? Would your good debt turn into bad debt if interest rates were to rise or your circumstances were to change? Always pay off your bad debt first.

We recognize there are financial challenges to being single or planning for a scenario in which you might be single once again. But information is power and so is confidence. Regardless of your present relationship status, you should be feeling doubly empowered to move forward on your journey to financial independence as a single, or potentially single, woman. In Part 2 we're moving from the general to the specific, from how to set yourself up for success to how to put the pieces in place to get you there.

PART 2

YOUR DREAM

BUILDING A FIRM
FOUNDATION

Chapter **5**

PLANNING FOR SUCCESS

You are a planner, although you may not realize it. Planning is natural. Everyone plans to some extent. Most people plan unconsciously or routinely for things, like what to have for dinner, when to meet up with friends and where to go on vacation. Just as we apply our planning skills to be able to make the most of our life today, we need to apply these skills to make the most of our future.

Planning is a bridge between your reality today and your future. Sometimes life just happens—many things occur in life without us planning on them happening. But for the most part, your financial situation happens because of your actions. Where you are today and where you will find yourself tomorrow are directly related to your planning or lack of planning. The more intentional you are about your finances, the greater chance you will have of achieving not only financial security but also of attaining financial independence.

Unfortunate things can happen as a consequence of not planning. For example, having to work longer before being able to retire; not being able to maintain the lifestyle you're used to; or not being able to help your kids with their education as you had really hoped to do, resulting in them having to take on student debt. These sorts of less-than-desirable outcomes are sometimes the result of circumstance, but far more often they are consequences of not planning.

A good plan is all-encompassing. For that reason, this chapter is full of considerations and, at times, may seem like a lot of work. But, trust us, the effort is more than worth it. By taking the time to plan, you are preparing for the best while also considering negative circumstances that might impact your future. We all have unexpected events in life, and we all have events that are inevitable. But leaving everything to chance is not the solution. A solid plan puts you in control and allows room for unforeseen circumstances, minimizing the impact of the unexpected.

A good plan also starts early. The earlier you start, the more choices you have and the more likely you are to achieve your ultimate goals. Your plan should also be written down and have clear steps outlined for achieving it. It must be put to work, with the right people on your side to help support you in making it happen. And, very importantly, it cannot sit on a shelf collecting dust. It is a living document that should change as your life changes.

For women, it is especially important to prepare for the future. Financial independence is not just about getting by; it is about being able to enjoy spending time with the people we love and doing the things that bring us joy. It's about being comfortable living the life we want while not having to worry too much about money. But the reality is, on average, women live longer than men; we tend to earn less than men; and our lives generally costs more than men's (haircut, anyone?). Add to all this the fact that many of us will be single in retirement, with one income, one set of government benefits, one pool of savings. All the more reason to plan carefully on the financial front. Your financial future is on you, even if you are not currently single. It is your responsibility to ensure that you can live a comfortable life for your entire life. And that takes planning.

A RICH LIFE IS ABOUT MORE THAN JUST MONEY

Before we can get to making your perfect plan, we need to establish the right mindset and acknowledge that life is about more than just dollars in the bank. We cannot lose sight of that. Relationships, interests and experiences are a few of the non-financial riches that bring us joy and fulfill our lives. You do not want a life that is rich financially but poor in other areas, nor do you want to be poor financially despite being rich in many other ways. Take inventory of all your riches. Having a truly rich life involves balance. For example, you may want to postpone paying off your mortgage by a year if it means enjoying a trip to celebrate a special event. Just make sure you can manage doing both.

Plans need to be flexible enough to allow responsibly for enjoying and celebrating things like those special events today. The great thing about a good plan is you can make decisions like this with confidence; and, because you had a plan in the first place, with some minor tweaks to it you can still stay on track. Money can provide more options for joy. Anything that can make your life richer that requires money definitely requires planning.

In her practice, Leslie sees just how frequently plans change and adapt. For example, for many people approaching retirement, all they really care about is retirement. They want to retire and be comfortable for their lifetime. Their financial legacy isn't of importance to them. Often, however, about three years or so into retirement, suddenly, leaving a financial legacy becomes a little more important to them and a topic they want to address. Your plan will evolve depending on life events and changing circumstances and priorities. Once you have a plan, review it at least once a year to monitor your progress toward your goals as well as any changes in your situation, and adjust your plan accordingly.

LOOK FORWARD TO YOUR FUTURE

Remember, having a vision for your future helps build confidence. It is the first step in building your plan, and a very important one. What are some of your personal hopes, dreams or goals that you want to accomplish? Who are the people that matter most in your life? What interests do you have? These are the things that bring us satisfaction and joy, and they are often closely aligned with our personal values.

Leslie would say "family" is one of her core values. Many of her personal goals and financial decisions revolve around her family, such as taking breaks from a busy career to spend dedicated time with family on vacation, buying a home in a family-friendly neighbourhood or providing a solid education for her children. And even for her retirement, it's important to Leslie to be able to maintain her current lifestyle and still have enough money to leave a meaningful financial legacy to her children.

Ardelle would say that one of her personal values is "independence." Many of her personal goals and financial decisions—whether they relate to her education, career pursuits or interest in real estate—have related to being able to live an independent life (not necessarily a solo life, but most certainly an independent one). It has always been important to her that she can support a comfortable lifestyle both during her working years as well as throughout her lifetime, without having to worry about money and never having to rely on others for it.

Often, our goals are a direct result of our values. These values may shift over the course of a lifetime, but seldom do our core values change radically from year to year. At a minimum, our goals need to align with our values to be meaningful and attainable. Because if your goals are not in line with your values, then you likely will not be able to keep up the motivation to make them happen

A plan starts with what matters to you. What are you most passionate about? These are the things that will allow you to persevere in the face of challenges and keep going in pursuit of success. It's like someone with a dream of becoming a doctor. There are many successful and renowned physicians who didn't get into medical school the first time they applied. However, they may have received valuable feedback, which helped strengthen their application the next year and ultimately helped them when they reapplied. By continuing to pursue their goal, they may have had to wait, but eventually their patience and perseverance paid off and they attained their dream.

There are those for whom retirement is a dream that they look forward to, and they avidly plan for the lifestyle they want. The goal of a comfortable, fulfilling retirement drives their financial decisions, the sacrifices they make along the way to attain that dream, and even their day-to-day actions and choices. Their retirement dream is their pole star, the beacon that guides their financial journey. For others, retirement isn't necessarily a dream but more of an inevitability. If something is an inevitability, it can be less of a motivator and more something you save for because you know you should. That can be dangerous. It then becomes easier for you to take from "retirement savings" to pay for short-term things like paying off a credit card or paying for a nice vacation. Or it may mean that you aren't motivated to save enough from year to year to ultimately be able to retire comfortably.

If you think retirement is an inevitability rather than a goal that's worth planning for, think of the things you enjoy doing today—for example, living in your home; enjoying that latte, manicure, vacation; driving your car; or buying a new pair of shoes. Imagine tomorrow you can't do any of those things. Just because you may not yet be able to envision your retirement, or you think it is too far away to be concerned about and it is just one of those things that eventually will happen, don't think you don't need to plan for it anyway. Let the fear of not being able to do the things you enjoy be your motivation.

If your plan includes the things that bring you joy, your vision for your future, as well as preparing for the inevitable, it also needs to consider those circumstances that you aren't planning on but that could possibly impact your finances. Life is full of surprises and, although you can't plan for them, you need to be prepared for them.

There are positive unexpected things that can happen to us, like promotions, the sale of a business for more than expected or possibly an inheritance. These are all events and resources that could improve your financial situation. But they can't be counted on. When it comes to planning, we cannot count our chickens before they hatch! Be aware of the possibilities, but don't rely on them.

There are also potential negative outcomes: needing to support or care for an aging parent, a disabled sibling, a dependent child or one who boomerangs home; or needing to adjust to job loss or business troubles, for example. These potential commitments and setbacks need to be considered not only as part of your planning process, but also as part of making big decisions, like choosing when to retire.

Before Ardelle retired, as an only child she considered whether she might need to provide financial support to her mom as her mom aged and, if so, whether she would be able to do so on her retirement income. Fortunately, Ardelle's mom, a widow, was open to having that discussion. It turned out that her mom had adequate resources and Ardelle could focus on just having to provide for herself. The worst-case scenario doesn't always come to pass, but it's a good idea to consider it in your planning process.

TIME IS MONEY

In today's world and in our society, time is a precious commodity. We all have tremendous pressures put on our time. But that isn't an excuse not to plan, especially because the process doesn't have to take a lot of time. If you are time-pressured or don't have the interest in actually running the numbers and creating a plan for yourself, there are experts who can help. Leslie often says she needs just three hours of a client's time (and much more of her own time!) to establish a plan:

- Initially, 1.5 hours to discuss your life, where you are today and where you want to be tomorrow.

- Followed by 1.5 hours to review the plan together and establish a go-forward strategy to make it happen.

If you are open and honest with an expert, she can actually do the planning and come up with strategies for you. Who doesn't have three hours to get a plan in place with a professional's help? The best part is that even if you don't have all the answers, you can simply start with those you do have. Your plan will evolve (they always do!). The main thing is to begin planning. Without fail you will be better off for at least having a plan, even if it is an evolving one.

So, let's not use the time factor as an excuse not to plan. This investment of your time has a guaranteed return: you will be well ahead of where you would have been without a plan! According to a longitudinal study by the Financial Planning Standards Council, titled *The Value of Financial Planning*, those with a comprehensive plan are almost twice as likely to report feeling on track with their financial affairs than those with no plan. Those with a comprehensive plan are more confident in their plan for retirement; are on track for their savings; feel better able to handle the bumps in the road of life, such as financial emergencies and tough economic times; have a strong sense of well-being; and, very importantly, feel that they can actually live and enjoy life today.[11]

It's clear that a small investment of your time now can have a profound impact on your overall well-being not just tomorrow but today as well. As you continue reading this chapter, if it starts to get a little overwhelming, remember: you can choose to do it on your own or you can choose to work with a knowledgeable advisor who will do the heavy lifting for you.

Time is indeed valuable. In fact, the sooner you start planning your finances, the better off you will be. The longer your timeline is for reaching your goals, the more choices you will have and the more strategies that will be available to you to help you meet your goals. Of course, retirement is the big one that starts out as a longer-term goal for many people to achieve at some date far in the future, but retirement in and of itself is for the long term! For a married couple in their mid-fifties to mid-sixties today, there is a 50-percent chance at least one of them will live to ninety-two.[12] Women's life expectancy today is in the low to mid-eighties—but remember, this is just an average and, as previously stated, the fastest-growing age demographic is people over the age of one hundred.

And so, if you retire at fifty-five, it could be the start of a phase of life that's thirty years long, or more, during which time you will most likely be needing your own savings to help carry you through. That takes planning, which in turn requires saving toward making your plans happen. The more time you have, the better able you will be to achieve success. The earlier you start, the more you will be able to accumulate to support a long, active retirement, as Table 5.1 illustrates. The table shows the total retirement savings for a woman at age sixty-five, depending on the age she starts saving, assuming she saves $10,000 each year and realizes a 7-percent annual return.

TABLE 5.1: It Pays to Start Saving Sooner

FROM AGE	SAVINGS AT AGE 65
25	$1,996,351
35	$944,608
45	$409,955
55	$138,164

The point is, we cannot put off planning for the long term. This means, there are no excuses for not planning—no claiming that life might change, that your income today may be different tomorrow, that your marital status might change or that where you live might change. Because the thing is, you are right: your life might change and, in fact, it most likely *will* change. As your circumstances change over time, your plans and goals might change accordingly, and so will your financial plan.

Those who plan accumulate more wealth. As Leslie has seen in her practice, this means that those with a plan are in a better financial position when life changes than those who failed to plan in the first place; they have more options and can reallocate their accumulated wealth as needed to achieve their revised goals and action plans. Starting early on your financial plan will not only give you a better chance of becoming financially independent, it will also make you more financially resilient.

BE SINGLE AND SAVVY

As we were researching and writing this book, one theme came up a few times: we heard from several single women that they had put off financial planning because they thought they might get married one day. While some didn't think this way intentionally, they said that, looking back to when they were younger, they didn't start really saving until they realized that they may actually never get married and it suddenly dawned on them, "This really is all on me!" That got them to start taking their finances seriously.

We saw a similar deferral tactic in women who were nearing retirement but were putting off planning how to generate their retirement income in the most tax-efficient way because they thought they might get married and it would change everything. Why would you compromise your own future for a partner who may never materialize? Or, revisiting an idea we mentioned earlier, who do you think might be more attractive to a potential mate: a woman who has her financial act together or one who doesn't? If you are single and you are wanting to get married, there is only upside to having your financial act together.

Ardelle never really planned on being single all her life, but she was prepared to be. She didn't delay getting started with her own planning. She never waited for Prince Charming to come along before she began saving and investing. Rather, she planned for her life as it was: she was the only income earner for the foreseeable future and it was on her to provide herself with a comfortable lifestyle. Regardless of her marital status, she was going to move forward with her financial goals while she continued to date. Because Ardelle didn't put off dealing with her finances and she planned for her life as it was, she was able to travel, study at a post-graduate level and retire comfortably and early. Had she put off planning, she wouldn't have started working toward her goals until it was too late, and she would still be working today.

Women who don't plan and therefore haven't really been accumulating dedicated financial resources, are all that much further behind when life does change. What you can't afford to do is put off starting. The more time you give yourself to save for your long-term goals, the more options you will have and the greater chance you will have of being able to maintain a comfortable lifestyle for your lifetime. Those who plan and start saving early, even just small amounts, are more likely to be able to retire at an earlier age. Not only do they have a longer time to put their money to work for them, but early on they also identify the values and goals that are most important to them and develop lifelong savings habits to support those long-term goals. Women who wait to start planning and saving for retirement often need to work longer and can find it much more challenging to achieve their dreams.

We've been talking a lot about not waiting until the right person comes along to start planning. But what if you are already married or in a committed relationship? Well, the same truisms about time and planning apply. The earlier you start your financial plan as a couple, the better off you'll be financially. But when doing your financial planning, you do need to remember the inescapable fact that, as a woman, there is a 90-percent chance you will end up on your own. This means that as you plan for a long, healthy and happy life together, you must ensure that what you are preparing for will still be comfortably achievable should you end up on your own. As we've said before, a significant proportion of marriages and common-law relationships end in divorce or separation. As part of your plan together, make sure you are saving and paying down debt. In the event of relationship breakdown, assuming there are no prenuptial agreements or cohabitation agreements, your assets after liabilities are split. The less debt, and the more savings, the greater the amount each of you will receive. Also make sure your family has the right amount of disability and life insurance to fill the gap caused by the loss of one income, one set of government benefits and, potentially, part of a pension. Plan as the happy couple you are today, but protect yourself in case life changes.

So far, we have talked about planning for people with some time before they retire. If you are in the age group approaching retirement, planning doesn't just involve savings and investing, it also starts to involve turning the financial resources you've accumulated into income in your retirement that will be tax efficient and last as long as you do. There are strategies about when it's best to start taking government benefits and when to withdraw from various types of investment accounts. Single or partnered, these are all important decisions in making the most of your financial resources and, like other aspects of planning, the earlier you start to plan your retirement income, the better off you will be. This kind of planning should start well before you actually retire, and planning ahead can have a very big impact on your income during your lifetime. Again, we know that time is a valuable commodity, but planning doesn't have to take much of your time if you choose to engage an advisor who will do the heavy lifting for you.

YOUR PLAN MUST BE WRITTEN DOWN

A good plan is a written plan and is SMART (specific, measurable, attainable, realistic and timely). You need to be able to refer to it, monitor your progress against it and to check in and make sure it still reflects your situation and objectives. Creating a plan is also a way to hold yourself accountable. Achieving your goals is on you, especially if you are single. Even if you are planning with your partner, you both need to be involved in the process. Putting your plan in writing will increase the likelihood of you committing to it and sticking to it.

For those of you who like visuals, you might even want to take things one step further and put pictures beside your goals. Sometimes referred to as a vision board, this kind of graphical representation of your dreams can make them seem more real and attainable for you. Pictures help us to envision the goal and to feel the emotion that we think we will actually feel when we achieve it. For example, say you want to buy a new home. Put a picture of your dream home beside your written goal of buying a new home, and when you look at it imagine how you will feel when you walk through the front door for the first time. Or perhaps put a picture of a bonfire beside the goal of paying off your mortgage, to symbolize burning your mortgage papers. How will you feel if you see your child graduate from the university you've been helping her pay for? Visually represent that goal and that feeling in your written plan. If one of your goals is retirement, imagine celebrating that milestone and enjoying the time it will allow you to focus on the people, activities and interests that bring you joy. Try finding pictures to represent these long-term dreams and goals. Pictures tell a thousand words and are more powerful than written words alone. Adding pictures to your specific written goals will give you increased motivation. When the going gets tough, they will give you the drive to persevere.

Ardelle ran a marathon in memory of her late father, as part of a charity fundraiser. Her long-range goal was overwhelming, as was the training at times, but all the planning and preparation she did were so worth it and made it possible for her to reach her goal. To be able to cross the finish line, which was her longer-range goal, she had to meet weekly milestones, which were her more realistic short-term goals. She would log her training runs in a journal so that she could map out her distance and endurance and see the progress she made weekly. To help motivate her during training and on race day, she carried in her waist belt a picture of her father and a small silver heart symbol that had significant meaning for her. Identify your best motivator, be it pictures, drawings, images, symbols, written objectives, sayings or journal entries. Making your financial plans and dreams happen is the longest marathon anyone could ever participate in. We'd argue it is also one of the most rewarding races you will ever run.

A GOOD PLAN GIVES YOU STRATEGIES

A good written plan includes not only your goals but also the strategies and individual actions that will get you there; the concrete steps that you need to take to make your plans work.

Strategies in a financial plan include:

- Choosing the right type of savings and investment accounts to use (different types of accounts have different tax implications).

- Determining which investments are best suited for you to achieve your goals.

- Identifying and pursuing any unique strategies that relate to your personal situation.

Concrete steps you need to take include things like:

- Figuring out how much you need to save to achieve a specific goal and setting out a schedule to accomplish that target.

- Targeting the rate of return you need to average on your investments over the long term to achieve your savings goals.

- Deciding to sell your business at some point and determining to what extent you need to grow that business in order to make your plans a reality.

- Deciding when you will buy that vacation home and how much is it going to cost.

It is relatively easy to determine the steps for short-term goals that have a specific dollar need associated with them. For instance, if your goal is to save $100,000 in five years to put down on the purchase of real estate, the steps are pretty clear. Because five years is a relatively short period of time, you should assume a more conservative rate of return, say just 3 percent to be safe. There is computer software that can calculate for you how much you need to save each year; or your financial advisor should be able to tell you that, to have the required $100,000 in five years assuming a 3-percent rate of return, you need to be saving $18,835 per year. Your concrete steps, then, are: Save $18,835 each year, in an investment strategy with a target annualized return of 3 percent. If you work with a financial advisor whose service offering includes planning, she will help by telling you the amount you need to save, recommend the right investment strategy and, ideally, help keep you on track to reach that goal.

Now, when it comes to long-term financial planning (i.e., retirement), that is often harder for people to plan. For most parts of a retirement plan, there are reasonable assumptions that can be used for factors like life expectancy, inflation, rates of return and your income sources, such as government benefits, pension income, rental property income and so on. The hardest part for many people when it comes to planning their retirement is determining how much you are likely to spend each year in retirement. There are rules of thumb based on a percentage of your working income, but Leslie has found in her professional practice that most people aren't average. They are unique and, as such, have their own specific needs and goals, to which you cannot simply apply a rule of thumb. Her advice for determining how much you will spend in retirement is to use the formula shown on page 70.

Once you've calculated the retirement income you'll need by following this formula, then it's time to determine how much you need to be saving each year to attain your goal. There is retirement planning software available that will help with this, and of course financial advisors who do planning work will be able to do this for you.

Calculating Your Retirement Spending

INCOME:
Start with your *after-tax* income today

EXPENSES:
Subtract: expenses that go away when you retire (e.g., commuting costs, work wardrobe, mortgage paid off, kids are out of the house and—a big one—you don't have to save regularly for retirement anymore!)

Add: new life expenses (e.g., increased travel, interests/hobbies, dining out, club memberships, courses and other adventures)

RESULT:
A pretty good idea as to how much you are going to spend in retirement.

The steps you need to take are the following:

1. Determine how much you expect to spend (using the formula in the box above).

2. Identify when you ideally want to retire.

3. List your current financial resources.

With this information, the amount you need to be saving can be calculated. This approach prioritizes your being able to maintain a certain lifestyle throughout your lifetime.

Another approach looks at retirement planning from a different perspective: If I am saving this much and I want to retire at this age, how much will I be able to afford to spend in retirement? In this case, again, you can do the work or you can have your advisor do it for you.

Regardless of your approach to retirement planning, a good advisor will take the information you give them and, based on your personal situation, help to identify those unique opportunities that you might have to improve your plans. For example, your advisor might counsel you not just on tax efficiencies to be gained on savings and investments but also advise you on how choosing a certain start date to collect your pension can affect your taxes and government benefits. Not only can she help by identifying opportunities to improve your plan, she can also assess the potential risks, which is a vital part of the planning process. Insurance options may need to be part of the conversation as a strategy to protect your ability to achieve your goals. (A full discussion of insurance will follow in Chapter 7.)

KEEP YOUR PLAN HANDY

What good is a plan if it sits on a shelf collecting dust? We'd say that would make it pretty useless. Unfortunately, that seems to be what happens to most financial plans. You plan once, the plan goes on a shelf, you blink, five years go by, and you might start thinking, "Did I ever actually do what that plan said I needed to do? What was it that I needed to do, anyway?" If you don't review and update it, you haven't got a clue if you are on track or not, let alone being able to benefit from the confidence a financial plan can provide.

A proper plan needs to stay relevant. You need to monitor your progress regularly to see if you are still on track. That is what your annual meeting with your advisor is all about. Or, if you are doing it on your own, you should set specific dates to review this information regularly yourself. Knowing that you are on track is what gives you confidence that you are in good shape to be able to enjoy a comfortable life, now and in the future. And if you're not completely on track, regularly checking your progress against your plan will enable you to make adjustments and get back on the rails before it's too late.

PLANS MEAN NOTHING WITHOUT ACTIONS

Now, keeping on track and making your plans your reality also implies that you are taking the necessary actions to make things happen. The strategies you decided to follow as part of your plan dictate what those actions are. But so many things in the financial world are beyond your control—economic trends, interest rates, movements of the stock markets and so on. Therefore, you will have to base your financial plan on reasonable assumptions for things like rate of return, inflation and your life expectancy. You might be able to influence the actual outcomes of these assumptions by the choices you make. For example, living a healthy lifestyle may enhance your life expectancy; the amount of risk you choose to take in your investments will impact the rate at which your investments grow over the long term; and you have some choice as to how much your expenses increase or decrease over time. However, for each of the assumptions you make, you can't fully control the outcome. And the actual results can have a significant impact on your ability to achieve your goals. In fact, the longer your time horizon, the greater impact even just a small variance from plan can have—positive or negative. That's another reason why check-ins are so important: they can help you make adjustments that account for the things you can't control.

Your actions need to be aligned with your plans and strategies, but you also need to adapt them from time to time in response to changing economic conditions outside of your control. Are you following an investment strategy that can reasonably achieve the rate of return you need over the long term, according to the assumptions you made in your plan? What are your actual longer-term returns compared to plan? At what rate are your expenses actually going up? Is the income goal you set in your plan still relevant today? To make your plans happen, you have to check in regularly and ask these kinds of questions. If things go off track, the sooner you know and the sooner you can make necessary changes. Monitoring your progress against plan regularly is one way to manage and respond to the forces you can't control, and it will make it easier for you to get back on track.

Because there are so many things in the financial world that are out of your control, it's extremely important to take action on the things you *can* control—for instance, implementing regular savings strategies using the account types that make the most sense for you. Or it could mean taking advantage of an opportunity to enhance or protect your plans, or following a strategy that makes sense for your particular circumstance. For example, Leslie often recommends to clients that they diversify their investment portfolio to reduce risk. It is common prudent advice, and yet it is amazing how much exposure some people have to their employer's stock, for instance. In many cases, not only are you working for Company X or drawing a pension from them, you may also receive stock options as a benefit and you hold that same company's stock in your investment portfolio, sometimes even unwittingly as part of your exchange-traded funds or mutual funds. In a case like that, far too much of your financial future is dependent on the fortunes of one company. If things go well for that firm, it's great for your net worth; but if things don't go as well as expected, your financial plans could very quickly be derailed. If you have too much invested in one stock or options of that same stock (including employment or retirement income), it might be wise to sell a portion of your investments that are linked to your employer, especially if you are nearing retirement (in about ten years or less).

Leslie learned this lesson many years ago when a colleague of hers retired. He had significant stock in a very well-respected Canadian company that paid a dividend that was considered "secure." Within weeks of his retirement, there was a major scandal and his retirement savings dropped 40 percent almost overnight. There are countless former Fortune 500 companies that at one time were considered indestructible, but don't exist today. Your biggest asset is your ability to earn an income. Be careful linking a significant portion of your savings to that very same source of income! If you realize you need to diversify your portfolio, then decide to sell part of that stock and do it. You have to follow through with it. What good is a plan or strategy you agree with if you don't put it into action?

At an even more basic level, your financial "habits" are actions that are completely within your control and you need to be very mindful of them. The everyday decisions you make about how you live your life impact your ability to make your long-term plans happen. These choices can include things like sticking to your budget and living within your means. One participant in our focus groups, a very successful career woman, said she always prepared and planned for the potential negatives, such as a job loss. That was her habit; she never counted on the positive, such as a raise. She did not want to ever have to rely on such nice financial surprises to keep her head above water. She lived, planned and saved for the long term based on her present income, never relying on receiving bonuses or promotions. As her career evolved and her income increased, rather than having to pay off debt from living large, she was able to improve her lifestyle as well as increase her savings for an improved retirement lifestyle.

One financial habit that many people put into action is paying yourself first: when a paycheque comes in, automatically save a portion of it first, then spend from what's left. And if you get a raise, first increase those regular automatic savings, then spend. Others choose to live off one source of income and save another. For instance, live off your regular earnings and save any bonuses and/or overtime pay or your income from a part-time job.

It's essential to start your financial planning with a vision of your future and to come up with appropriate strategies to accomplish your goals. But plans without action are just dreams. Don't be just a dreamer, be the author of your own financial destiny; take action and make your vision of financial independence happen.

Create a Great Plan Based on Your Vision for Your Future

- Identify your short- and long-range goals.
- Designate time to plan.
- Choose concrete strategies to get you there.
- Identify the action steps you need to take.
- Consider circumstances beyond your control that might impact you financially.
- Track your progress.
- Be flexible; your plan will change as your life changes.
- Celebrate all successes!
- And remember, you don't have to do it on your own.

THE ROAD IS LONG,
BUT THE JOURNEY FLIES BY

Everyone knows the expression "Time flies." While that may be true of time, the road to a long-term goal can feel daunting at the start. Like paying off that mortgage in twenty-five years. Twenty-five years! That seems like a long time. Or needing to save $2 million to retire comfortably (if that is the amount you need to be comfortable), but you have just $750,000 now. Long-term objectives, such as paying off your mortgage or saving for your retirement, all involve taking little steps. Small everyday actions now can have a huge impact on your outcome. One day you will look back and hardly believe that when you first started toward your goal you didn't know how you would do it. Henry Ford said, "Whether you think you can, or you think you can't—you're right." You can do it. Start small, stick to your plan and increase your efforts when you are able. Breaking your big goal down into smaller steps and milestones will build your confidence and motivate you to achieve the goals you plan for. And don't forget to celebrate the small victories along the way!

Chapter 6

BUDGETING IS NOT A BAD WORD

Budgeting is the art of enjoying living life today and being responsible about tomorrow. Make no mistake about it—we are not asking you to sacrifice everything today for some day way down the road. Life is for living. But you also need to remember that your older self is relying on your younger self to live life in a financially responsible way.

Regardless of your age, marital status or income, you know that spending less than you make is the right thing to do. But that's not all there is to budgeting. It's also about knowing what you spend money on, so that you can plan for the future. Consider this: You are at a stage of life during your working years when your bank account and cash flow are well in hand. You're saving and feeling good about your future. But you are tired. Tired of the work treadmill, feeling like it is time for a career change, but not sure what's next. For many people, taking a sabbatical, or going back to school for a career change, is the answer. But how can you plan financially for a loss of income for a period of time, if you don't know how much you spend?

What if, instead of being mid-career, you are nearing the end of your working life and looking forward to retirement? How can you possibly know whether or not you are on track to achieve financial independence in retirement, if you don't know how much you spend? Retirement is a long phase of life, during which your assets have to support your spending. How would you know if your assets are sufficient to generate the income stream you need to retire comfortably for your lifetime, if don't know how much your lifestyle costs? Tracking spending is the only way to know. As you read the word "budget" (or "spending plan") many times in this chapter, remember our definition: it is the art of balancing enjoyment today with being responsible about tomorrow. Budgeting isn't a negative thing; it simply is the only way to accomplish both.

Budget by Another Name: Call It What You Want

Some people have a negative reaction to the word "budget." The barriers come up, and the excuses come out. When some people hear the word, they immediately draw a negative association (e.g., restriction, limit, constraint) rather than a more positive connotation (e.g., blueprint, strategy, plan). If you don't like the word budget, then substitute your own word or phrases that you can buy into. If cooking is something you enjoy, instead of calling your budget your "budget," call it your financial recipe. Or if you like sports, you can call it your game plan. Perhaps it is simply your spending plan. Whatever you do, don't let the dislike of a simple word hold you back from doing what you know is right.

A budget does not limit you; rather, it is a plan that puts you in control, because it is designed by you and is unique to you and your personal circumstances. You get to make choices based on your priorities, and you get to be in control of your money by gaining insight into your spending and saving. Your budget has to support your goals and fit with your values; in this way, it can help ensure that you have the money to spend on what you want most. A financial plan will tell you how much you need to be saving to achieve the things that matter most to you, but it is your budget that allows you to save and, therefore, it is critical to your ability to achieve the ultimate goal: financial independence.

YOU CAN'T ALWAYS GET WHAT YOU WANT

What is a need and what is a want? Only you can decide. But be warned: We all can rationalize anything as being a need if it is something we really want and if we aren't honest with ourselves. For instance, we all need a roof over our head. For some people, a large home in the best neighbourhood may truly be affordable, and for many perfectly good reasons it might be the right housing solution. Others need a home, and they can come up with a million reasons why that house in *the* neighbourhood is simply perfect for them; however, for them, "affording" it would be at the expense of being able to set aside any savings at all, and it may mean an exceptionally long mortgage payoff schedule (or amortization period). They may have convinced themselves they "need" that house but, really, it is more of a want. This process of rationalizing a want into a need is how many people get themselves into trouble—living a lifestyle they cannot afford. They may be living life today, but they are definitely not being responsible about tomorrow.

We all have wants. But how many of them can you really afford? It's all about choices and priorities. If it is a want, does it fit with your values? Earlier we talked about values and how they should shape your financial goals. Nowhere else can your values have more influence than on your budget and what you choose to spend money on. If your goals are shaped by what you truly value, meaning those things that bring you joy, and if you consider your value assessment when you budget, it will help you make wise spending decisions and choices whether you are single or with a partner. Your spending habits—the things that you choose to spend your money on, or not, each and every single day—actually dictate whether or not you can save enough to achieve those very goals.

A spending plan will help you assess your daily choices against your long-term goals and values. It will allow you to decide what you value more: eating out tonight, or travelling to Europe next year? Driving the ultra-luxe car today, or enjoying a home in a better climate for six months a year in retirement? That new purse and matching shoes today, or helping your kids afford university in a few years? Or maybe you place high value on going to the theatre, or some other experience or activity, and so you do make the choice to enjoy it today.

The point is, if you can articulate your values, set your goals based on those values and evaluate your spending decisions in light of them, it can be the most powerful influencer on your financial decisions today. Aligning your budgeting and day-to-day spending decisions with your long-term financial and lifestyle goals will give you the strength and resolve to live responsibly today so you can achieve your vision for the future you want.

YOU CAN'T COUNT ON THE LOTTERY WIN

As we have stated before, you can't count on winning the lottery to solve your money problems. The odds of winning Canada's Lotto Max are approximately one in 28.6 million. But someone's got to win, right? Unfortunately, a shocking number of people are relying on it. A Bank of Montreal survey found that 34 percent of Canadians believe winning the lottery will fix their retirement problems.[13] Fourteen percent are counting *heavily* on the win. And the long-odds lottery win isn't the only windfall that people are counting on—40 percent are counting on an inheritance. Again, they are effectively relying on someone else to get them out of what would otherwise be a difficult situation.

Inheritances are never guaranteed: wills can be changed on a whim, a remarriage can change everything and health care costs can erode what once may have been a sizable estate. Until that money is in your hands, it cannot be relied upon. Count an inheritance as a bonus, as a possible means of improvement or an unexpected windfall that can accelerate the realization of your goals—but under no circumstances should you budget for an inheritance in your financial plan, any more than you should an extremely unlikely lottery win. You simply cannot count your chickens until they hatch! It isn't hard to imagine that throughout the developed world shocking percentages of the population put themselves in these camps. And for women on their own, a lucky win or a legacy may seem like the only way to get ahead. But hope is not a strategy! Believe us when we say, you can't blindly bet your future on a jackpot, an inheritance or, like Cinderella, on finding a Prince Charming.

We hope you will choose instead to take matters into your own hands and create your own win. It doesn't matter if you are just getting started, or if you have already built significant wealth. Doing things like budgeting—knowing what you spend, spending less than you make, planning and learning when to adjust spending, or even sometimes saying no—may sometimes feel like a sacrifice in the moment, but the moment will pass. Making that tough choice in the short term will make the long-term rewards all the sweeter. If you step up, decide to be in control of your money, take control of your finances again or maybe for the very first time, your odds of success are far greater than if you choose to rely on the ever-elusive win instead.

YOU CAN COUNT ON YOURSELF AND YOUR ACTIONS

Some people naturally don't spend as much as their income allows. For them, their income comes in, they save money regularly into their investment accounts, and expenses go out. At the end of the month, they have more in their bank account than they had at the start of the month. For them, their "budget" is simply that their bank account keeps growing. Regardless how small or how large one's income is, these people are rare. For the rest of us, the tendency is to spend as much as you make, or more. Without some sort of expense-tracking mechanism and spending plan, it's easy to incur excessive expenses, which leads to excessive, debilitating debt that must be paid off before you can even contemplate enjoying living a life of financial independence. It's essential to have at least a rough budget to stay on track with your financial plan and your goals. A budget helps you gain an understanding of what lifestyle you can and cannot afford today, if you also want to afford the goals and the lifestyle you're dreaming of in the future.

For those who say, "I don't need to write it down to know I spend too much," we say, "Oh yes, you do!" You may not like having to record the facts or seeing the harsh reality on paper, but as the famous Nike saying goes, *Just Do It!* Not starting with this exercise is the equivalent of wanting to recover from an injury but not wanting to know about or do the exercises the physiotherapist recommends. The result is the same: you remain in pain, limiting your future ability and perhaps even hurting yourself more.

If you are single, no one can tell you what you can and can't spend your money on. It is up to you. You get to make all the choices—on how much to save and how much and on what you get to spend. If you are part of a couple, well, you get a say in what your household spends money on, but so does your partner. For those who are married, a budget is something you need to do together, and both be committed to in order to be successful. Generally, the degree to which couples share values, agree on goals and agree on budgets often translates to how they manage their bank accounts. For those very closely in tune with each other on these issues, joint accounts can be used to manage the household cash flow. Even if well-aligned, some couples choose to have separate accounts and split financial responsibilities. At the end of the day, either approach can work; it is personal choice. The issue of managing the household's cash flow becomes more important when a couple isn't on the same page, financially or otherwise, or if there is another major issue (e.g., when one partner is a spendthrift). In such cases, separate finances may be a better idea. Remember, 90 percent of women end up single. Even something like budgeting and how you manage your household's cash flow can be a very important tool for protecting yourself should you become one of the 90 percent.

BUDGETING 101

When it comes to a budget being effective, there are two universal truths:

- Universal Truth #1: You have to spend less than you make.

- Universal Truth #2 (for those in the working years): You have to save. Savings is a need, it is not an option or a luxury. You will never be financially independent if you don't save, invest and build wealth!

You don't need to be good at math or take a course or have a degree in finance to be good at budgeting. A budget is a tool that everyone should use, regardless of their financial situation or level of knowledge. Yes, a budget includes how much you spend on the basic costs of living like rent, mortgage, hydro and groceries, but you also need to plan to spend money on some rewards (treats, wants) as part of your budget. That's right—everyone's budget should accommodate not only being able to get by but also being able to enjoy life in the present. The key: these rewards need to be within your means. There are four simple steps to creating a realistic spending plan.

Step 1: Track All Personal Expenses and Spending

Seeing truly is believing! In general, people tend to underestimate how much they spend and overestimate how much they save. Tracking such details can be an eye-opener. You might just be shocked at how much you spend on eating out, for instance. Or, in some cases, you find out you really are doing well in some areas. Once everything is tracked, you can see and calculate how much money you spend and on what. There is no more assuming or guessing. Perhaps you see that you are able to save more than you thought toward a short-term goal. Or you realize that there are some expenses that you could choose to cut out or reduce. You may be spending money on items you don't use or get value out of. You get to decide and make these choices.

There are many tools available to help with this. With online banking and credit card accounts, you can download the transactions into a basic program like Excel, sort your expenses into different categories and simply add them up. Do this for a few months, and then start to notice the trends. If Excel isn't your thing, there are other software programs or apps, like Mint.com, that your online banking and bills will allow you to download directly to.

- Initial set-up time: about 2 hours

- Maintenance time: about 1 hour per month

Once you track your spending, if you find that after saving enough for both short-term and long-term goals, and after spending, at the end of the month you have more than you had at the beginning, you are in good shape; you have choice. You can choose to

- continue on without making changes; or

- accelerate some of your short-term goals and experience the freedom that comes with achieving financial independence, through finding ways to save even more.

One couple who were transitioning to retirement were evaluating their spending to make sure that their estimates of what they would need each year to be comfortable were right. They were amazed to see just how much they were spending on utilities. Part of their plan had always been to downsize their home. Once they saw their utility bills, they decided to build a home that would effectively enable them to live off the grid. It cost a bit more up front in the build, but it dramatically cut down their ongoing cost of living. Their plans were well in hand, but simply knowing what they were spending money on motivated them to modify those plans and, in the end, actually improved their long-term financial position. Similarly, Ardelle tracked her spending both before and after she retired to confirm that she could adjust her spending on a reduced income.

If, on the other hand, after saving and spending, at the end of the month you are short on funds, change is needed immediately. There are only two choices for a person who is living beyond her means and is in need of getting on to the right path: increase income or reduce expenses. Those are the only two options.

Step 2: Save!

For those in their working years, your first financial priority should be to save. Remember, saving is a need; it is not an option, nor is it a luxury. You will never achieve financial independence if you don't save. You may have heard the expression "Pay yourself first," which is generally considered the best piece of financial advice and the most effective way to build long-term wealth that anyone ever came up with. This is the part about being responsible today to improve your financial situation tomorrow. If you are or you become a disciplined saver now, your future self will thank the younger you.

Before any expenses come out, move some money into your savings and investment accounts and set it up to happen automatically like your other bills or necessary expenses. Out of sight, out of mind—if it isn't in your bank account, you will be less tempted to spend it. Take care of saving first; what is left covers your necessary living expenses, and everything over and above that becomes the disposable income you get to enjoy today.

If you have a savings plan available through work, not only can your savings be deducted automatically from your paycheque before the money even hits your bank account, but your employer may even match your savings! Imagine that: you save, and your employer matches the amount you set aside, or at least a portion of it. Where else are you going to get an instant guaranteed return of, say, 30 percent, 50 percent, or even 100 percent? Employer plans can sometimes have a different set of risks that need to be understood and addressed, but there are very few exceptions to the rule if they are going to match your contributions. Get the match and always take the free money!

Another great strategy for saving is living on one source of income and saving another source of income. So, for instance, live off your salary and save your bonus. Jay Leno has made public how he saved his income from *The Tonight Show* and relied on his other gigs to cover his expenses. This strategy is not for only the rich and famous. When Ardelle was saving for her first condo, a goal that was very much in line with her values of being financially secure and independent as well as her desire to own her own home, she eventually got to the point where she was saving all her income from her full-time employment while she lived off her part-time earnings.

Regardless of the strategy you use—whether you pay yourself first, live off of one income source and save another, a combination of both, or you employ another strategy that simply works for you—once you have taken care of saving first for what matters most to you, covering your necessary expenses and obligations (mortgage, utilities, taxes and so on), then what is left becomes the income you get to spend on enjoying today.

Step 3: Assess and Adjust

Now that you have tracked what you are actually spending money on, and you've set up your savings to be able to achieve your short- and long-term goals, you can now see if you are following the two universal budgeting truths or not.

If you are on the right track—you are saving for your short- and long-term goals, and you are spending less than what is left—you can choose to carry on. Or, you might just say to yourself, I really spend *that* much on *that*? If "that" isn't something you really value, or you don't really get much use or enjoyment out of it, you might just decide to make a change and choose to spend more on something else you truly value instead, or to enhance your savings. Even for those who go through the exercise and find they are in good shape, there potentially are opportunities to change and improve their circumstances.

On the other hand, if you have tracked your spending and saving and find you are spending beyond your means and racking up an ever-growing debt, then change is absolutely necessary. Change is always hard, but it is rewarding.

Step 4: Plan Your Spending

Failing to plan is planning to fail. (This saying is often attributed to Benjamin Franklin, among others, and has itself become a sort of universal truth.) Regardless of whether it is used to accelerate your ability to live a financially independent life, or to help you get your financial house in order, having a spending plan really is an essential step. You have taken the time to track your expenses and know what you have been spending money on. Now is the time to say, "Going forward, this is how much I am going to spend each month, on each budget line." Write down those amounts, such that the total you are planning to spend is less than the income you have available to spend.

Yes, you read that right: The goal should be to get to the point where—after saving for specific long-term goals like achieving financial independence or short-term wants and goals, like that bathroom reno or a special trip—the amount you plan to spend is *less* than the amount you have available each month. Life happens. Your budget needs to have room in it for those rainy days, to be able to handle life's unexpected events. The unexpected might not happen every month, but you can certainly count on it happening with at least some degree of frequency. By giving yourself room and allowing your bank account to accumulate funds over time, you give yourself the ability to handle challenges when life happens.

Just like your financial plan needs to be written, so does your spending plan. In Step 1: Tracking Your Spending, we recommended recording all your expenses either in Excel or using some other budgeting program or online tool. In that same program, you can also set your budget. Record what your budget for each line is. First, input the costs for fixed expenses, those amounts that you are obliged to pay every month and that really don't change. Some of these items may be negotiated or you can shop around for a better deal. For instance, cellphone bills, home internet, cable, insurances, monthly parking or groceries.

Also, very importantly, you need to set a budget for those expenses that bring you joy today—your rewards. Remember, budgeting is the art of balancing enjoyment today with being responsible about tomorrow. Hopefully your financial condition is such that if there is something that brings you joy, you are still able to do it, at least to some extent. Perhaps you enjoy going to the theatre or eating out. Hopefully you can still do those things, but be prepared that many times the things that bring you joy are where you may have to modify your spending; usually these are your entirely elective expenses, completely discretionary and, therefore, the first ones to get cut back. For instance, if travel is important to you, we want you to still be able to travel. You may just have to "modify" the extent of your travel. Perhaps this means shortening the length of your trips, going to less-expensive destinations or travelling less frequently.

For those who enjoy watching home renovation shows, you may have heard of the high/low strategy. It's when you spend a lot on one element of a room, but then spend less on another. This same high/ low strategy can be applied to any of your lifestyle choices. Sticking with the travel example, you might choose to save some money by taking a less expensive vacation one year, and then the next time you travel, a more expensive vacation like you may have been used to, followed by a less expensive vacation again. Or you may decide to drive instead of fly, but stay at a more expensive hotel in a great location. Making room for some level of discretionary spending (and, therefore, joy and rewards in your life) is all about trade-offs. Get creative with applying the high/low strategy to reduce the total cost of those things that bring you joy, so you can still balance being able to enjoy today while being responsible about tomorrow.

Once you have a written budget that shows how much (or how little) you can spend on each line item in any given time period (weekly, monthly, annually), you need to make sticking to your budget a priority and keep yourself accountable to it. Each week, download your banking and credit card transactions into the program you have chosen to use to set your budget and track your spending. You do need to keep on top of it. If you set your budget on a monthly basis, the more time that goes by from the start of the month to when you track expenses again, the more room there is to overspend and not even realize you are overspending. You may need a method for tracking expenses more frequently, so you can be aware of where you are financially in the moment and will be able to know if there is still room in the budget or not.

But let's face it, no matter how accurately you may have budgeted, it's way too easy to spend and overspend when you're wielding those powerful little pieces of plastic and not tracking expenses diligently. If you need a little more enforced discipline, put your debit card and credit cards away and use cash only (a.k.a. the envelope method). When you receive your paycheque, withdraw cash in the amount you are budgeting to spend in total, and allocate the cash across different envelopes, each one dedicated to a specific type of spending. Put so much for groceries in one envelope, so much for haircuts in another envelope, so much for gifts, eating out, and so on. Once the money in a particular envelope is gone, there is no more spending allowed until the next paycheque. This is probably the strictest method of budgeting and, in today's near-cashless society, may not be followed by many people in its purest form. However, there are now software programs that allow you to set your virtual "envelope budget" for various categories, and to download your bank account and credit card transactions so the program will actually do your envelope tracking for you.

Another modification to this method is one that Leslie and her family use. Like many people today, all their fixed expenses and costs for utility bills and so on are set to be deducted automatically from the bank account. Their discretionary spending is all done on a credit card (love those travel points!). Once the credit card hits the budgeted amount for monthly elective spending, that's it, it is cut off. No more spending on it until the next billing cycle.

The main thing is not only that you *set* your spending plan, but that you *track* yourself to that plan! Just like your financial plan needs to have a tracking mechanism to be successful, what good is a budget if you don't know if you are sticking to it or not?

Budgeting Is About More Than Just Expenses

Say the word "budget," and we all think expenses. But, in truth, a budget (or spending plan) is all about having enough income to support both saving and spending. Sometimes expenses aren't the problem, income is. If modifying the expense side of the ledger doesn't work, it may be time to explore ways to increase income.

SHOULD I SWEAT THE SMALL STUFF?

It depends. If your cash flow is well in hand, you may find that you don't have to sweat the small stuff. You may choose to, but you don't have to. On the other hand, if you aren't saving enough and you are living paycheque to paycheque—or worse, carrying or accumulating debt—then, yes, you really should be sweating the small stuff.

Start with not wasting money on things you don't use. Some people actually use their gym memberships; countless others feel good having one and always have the best intentions, but they never go.

If you don't go to the gym, don't pay the membership! Don't waste money on things you don't use.

Often, the little expenses add up. Just take a look at your credit card bill. There may be $20 here, $50 there, and then suddenly the bill comes and it amounts to thousands of dollars. Each of us may have that one habit that actually adds up to something meaningful each year. Let's look at the mani-pedi effect. Everywhere, in large cities and even small towns, there always seems to be a nail salon close by. If you like to stop into your local salon for a little pampering every now and again, what does that mean for your budget? Spending $50 every other week is $1,300 a year. Saving $1,300 per year for eighteen years at a 5-percent rate of return per year grows to a little over $36,500. If you value your children's education but just can't seem to find the funds to save toward it, but you have regular mani-pedis, which do you value more? The small stuff adds up. What is your mani-pedi effect? For some it is the classic daily latte fix; for others it's shoes, purses, lottery tickets or buying lunch every day. If you start to sweat the small stuff, you might just find ways to make your big stuff happen!

It takes time and energy, but shop around. A question Ardelle always asks herself is, *Could I do this in a less expensive way and still be happy?* Resourcefulness and curiosity drive her to find the answer. If you like wine, showing an expert at a wine or liquor store a bottle of wine you like and asking for recommendations for other similar-tasting wines can help you find a less-expensive option that you may enjoy just as much. And you could have a lot of fun trying to find your new favourite!

When it comes to travel, single people are always frustrated by having to pay pricey single supplements, especially on cruises. By shopping around and working with a good travel agent, though, you can find cruise companies that have more reasonable single supplements or have a few cabins on certain sailings that are reserved for singles with no additional single charge. Put out a little extra effort and work with the right travel professional, and you can still enjoy a great vacation without having to pay an unnecessary additional expense simply because you're single.

When single people need to make larger purchases, it helps to take someone else with you. For instance, a fake husband. Ardelle has "borrowed" a husband (but always returned him) as a means of getting a better price on certain purchases. Yes, it's frustrating that men and women and couples are treated differently by salespeople. And, yes, it's unfair that single women are often at a financial disadvantage as a result. But sometimes it is reality, and that is what we have to work with. Ardelle has found that when shopping for large purchases, such as appliances or home renovations, sometimes having a person with you who is male can lead to what she feels has been a better price than she would have gotten otherwise. Now, perhaps it is the ability to play "good cop/bad cop" or outnumbering the salesperson that helps; or perhaps it's that during a discussion different people pick up on specific negotiable points that can be used in your quest for either the best price or other terms of agreement. But the point is, if you are a single woman making large purchases, you might just want to try taking someone, especially a male, with you when the time for negotiation comes.

The bottom line is, think of budgeting not as a tedious, onerous chore but, rather, as a useful, simple tool to help you reach the financial goals you have set for yourself. Keep in mind that your budget is linked to the vision you have for your future, it's not just a boring task you have to do today. What do you value? Let that be your guide to helping you choose what you spend money on and what you don't— and be your ticket to financial independence.

Chapter 7

PROTECT YOURSELF, AND OTHERS YOU CARE ABOUT

If you are single, the responsibility for your well-being is solely yours. Sure, you have your network of friends and family, and maybe even some trusted professional advisors, to help you with important decisions and to counsel you when needed. But when it comes right down to it, you have to provide for yourself, both now and in the future, and no one cares about your money as much as you do. As such, you would be wise to think about protecting yourself, and there are all kinds of ways to do that. Our focus in this chapter is on protecting yourself financially.

The degree to which you will choose to protect yourself ultimately comes down to your priorities and your risk tolerance. Some risks, we are willing to take; there are other risks we aren't so willing to take; but the scariest risks are the ones we didn't even know we were taking.

FINANCIAL AWARENESS

In previous chapters we discussed the importance of being informed about where you stand financially, taking your financial inventory and being engaged in your financial journey. Taking responsibility to build your self-awareness in these ways is the first step to financial independence. Being informed doesn't just build confidence, it also protects you. Financial awareness helps you make better decisions and helps protect you from others in the event someone else might potentially cause you financial harm. The more aware you are of a situation, the easier it will be to spot a problem and be proactive about dealing with it.

Earlier, we used an example of a spouse or partner intentionally withholding information. Being fully aware of, and engaged in, your financial situation can help you avoid getting into that position in the first place, and give you security and protection should you eventually end up on your own. It can also prevent you from making poor choices or becoming a victim of white-collar crime. We are all familiar with stories of famous people, such as musicians or sports personalities, whose exceptional wealth disappears because of financial mismanagement by people they hired. And fraud, system hacks and identity theft have become everyday occurrences that can affect any of us.

Taking a little time to be informed is smart, prudent planning. But increasing your self-awareness when it comes to your own finances needs to become a daily habit. Constantly being aware of where you stand will make it easier for you to spot a financial problem or opportunity and be more proactive about dealing with it. It's easy to improve your financial IQ by reading and asking questions, not only of friends and family whose opinions you respect, but also of financial and legal professionals, depending on the circumstances. If you don't take that bit of time to invest in yourself, and if you aren't informed about your money matters or don't have some way of tracking your finances through time, you have little hope of seeing those warnings or those opportunities, let alone being able to do anything about them.

Being informed isn't just about building confidence by providing reassurance, it is also about being financially responsible and prudently managing your risks. Choosing not to be informed about your financial position is the equivalent of driving without insurance, or walking across a busy four-lane road in the middle of rush hour without looking both ways. You might agree these are risks that are foolish to take—you are asking for trouble if you don't anticipate them. Choosing not to be informed or protect yourself financially is effectively choosing to take risks you didn't necessarily even know you were taking. So, make the choice to be informed. Choose to be responsible. Not only will being informed protect you, it will also provide comfort and confidence—and quite possibly will also help you build more wealth and, therefore, a bigger safety net down the road.

So, in practical terms, how can building your financial awareness protect you? Perhaps it is a spending log or a financial review that shows you aren't saving as much as you should be, that your mortgage isn't being paid down as fast as it should, or how did that line of credit creep up, anyway? A financial inventory, keeping track of where you are, not just today but over many years and decades, can help protect your hard-earned finances. Being completely informed about your finances provides you with the opportunity to ask questions and to intervene early, before a problem becomes a real problem.

But being informed is not only about avoiding risk and preventing potential financial disaster. It also can help identify opportunities that can make a tremendous difference in your long-term financial health. For instance, if you notice that your bank balance is growing over time, but you're frustrated at how slowly the mortgage seems to be coming down, there is an opportunity to make some mortgage prepayments, ultimately saving you thousands of dollars in interest over the years. This opportunity can make a significant difference in your long-term financial well-being—becoming mortgage-free faster, building more equity faster and freeing up precious resources to invest in your financial future in other ways.

Leslie has observed a common trait of financially successful people: they have usually paid off the mortgage on their home faster than the standard twenty-five-year amortization schedule. They are purposeful and intentional about monitoring their finances on a regular basis to know where they stand, which helps to ensure that they have enough resources every year to make extra payments. There are other ways to improve your financial future simply because you are always aware of your circumstances and the numbers. For example, you might identify an opportunity because you realize that your savings account isn't really growing in this low-interest-rate environment, and this perhaps leads you to explore other investment opportunities whereby even a small improvement in return can make a tremendous difference in the long run.

Financial awareness makes you question the situation, and patterns may reveal themselves to you—both the potential negative situations you may find yourself in and the possible opportunities to make a positive impact. Avoiding negative situations and taking advantage of opportunities will both work to protect you. Minimize the effect of a negative situation early, and you won't find yourself in a hole that is hard to dig yourself out of in the future. Taking advantage of opportunities to improve your long-term financial well-being effectively builds in a cushion, another layer of resources and protection to draw from in the event of a job loss or a health issue that you or someone you love is faced with. Honing and relying on your financial intelligence can even help you to afford that cottage, travel or take a sabbatical. Being self-aware in money matters enables you to take advantage of the opportunities that information presents you with, and it protects you by giving you more financial resources to draw from. Such a simple strategy for protecting yourself, but it works!

LIFE EVENTS AND MAKING BIG DECISIONS

Being informed doesn't just apply to knowing where you stand from day to day or month to month with all your bank accounts, investments, financial plans and spending habits. It also applies to life's many changes and the big decisions you'll have to make along the way. Every major life event has financial implications, but not every decision in life can be made based solely on the numbers. We recognize that living a financially independent life means being smart about tomorrow, while also balancing that with being able to enjoy today. For example, choices you make in doing a renovation may incur costs that won't be recovered if you sell your home in the future, but those choices make a meaningful impact on your ability to enjoy your home today. If you can afford it, go ahead and do it. The key is, *if you can afford it.* Knowing that it isn't going to put your long-term financial health in jeopardy means first being informed about your current financial position, and also having an understanding of what the outcome may be.

On his fortieth birthday, Leslie's husband was asked what the most exciting thing was that had happened in his thirties. Well, in that decade alone, he and Leslie had celebrated the birth of two children, renovated two houses and moved once, and Michael had completed an Ivy League MBA and had four job changes. Needless to say, it was a busy decade (no wonder they felt tired!). Life happens, and sometimes it feels like it's happening in fast-forward. When major events come at you or you are faced with big life decisions, it's essential to be mindful of the full impact—qualitative and quantitative. For Leslie and Michael, and their whole family, all these life changes had a financial component.

For instance, the investment in an Ivy League MBA. The outcome wasn't assured, and the cost was high. There were many considerations to take into account—financial and non-financial—to make the right decision: the opportunities for reward that would come from having taken the risk of a major investment in his education. Yes, he and Leslie would have to take on debt to finance the MBA and there would be a major investment of Michael's time, both of which would impact short-term family goals. But, as a result, there would be the potential for increased income in the long run. Just as important as the improved financial prospects was the possibility of a more exciting career in an area Michael was, and still is, passionate about. Given the amount of time people spend at work, if you can be passionate about what you do and enjoy going to work every day, that should contribute to a happier life.

The key is to be mindful and intentional in your decision making. Don't just let life happen to you. Going with the flow can mean drowning in debt if you don't have a reasonable plan to pay for whatever financial obligations you take on; if there are unintended financial implications of a major life event; if the positives don't actually come to fruition; or if the rewards take longer to realize than you expected.

Planning for life events and informing yourself about realistic potential outcomes *before* you make decisions does take a bit of time, and it
takes some thought. But as with many things, the investment of your
time has a guaranteed return: protecting yourself in the future, and
the peace of mind that comes from that. You might not know what
the outcome of any decision or change in life will be, but at least you
can reassure yourself that taking the risk shouldn't lead to financial
hardship.

LOVE AND MONEY

One life change that can take some extra consideration from a financial point of view is marriage (including common-law unions).
Staying on top of your own finances is hard enough, and juggling
priorities for just one person is challenging—never mind when another person is in the mix. As tough as money conversations can
be, especially in those heady early days of a romance, you need to
protect your own interests and look out for one another. Financial
issues are a leading cause of breakups and divorce—so, protect your
relationship as well as your financial future by getting ahead of the
disagreements and conflicts over money!

It's essential before you enter into marriage to be fully informed
about your future spouse's finances—not only about what their assets are and if they have any big debts or financial obligations such
as spousal and child support—but also their attitudes about money,
about spending and about who controls the purse strings and makes
the financial decisions. And what about your goals? Do your goals as
individuals align? They don't all have to be the same, but you may
want to have full discussions about any that you are completely at
odds about!

These are important conversations. They can reaffirm that things
are good, or they can also raise some red flags ("Hang on a second,
how did he accumulate that much debt?"). Are you potentially marrying a spendthrift? If so, and you move forward in the relationship
anyway, what are you going to do to protect yourself? In this situation, there are things you can do to safeguard your position, like

maintaining separate accounts and limiting joint debt to just the mortgage or car payments. You may also want to ensure you have a marriage contract (a.k.a. a prenuptial agreement) that spells out who is responsible for any debt that's coming into the marriage along with your future spouse. The point is, by being informed, you can take the steps to protect yourself just in case.

Another red flag may actually be realizing, "You spend that little?" Yes, spending that little can be a red flag. Have you ever heard of a woman whose spouse won't let her have a credit card and has had the bank put a small daily limit on her debit card, effectively limiting her access to money? You might be shocked, but it happens. Informing yourself about your future partner's financial attitudes and habits is extremely important. It gives you the opportunity to make decisions and take steps to protect yourself and your future financial position should you need to.

Even if there are no red flags popping up when you take financial inventory and explore money issues together, it's a good idea to protect what each of you is bringing into the marriage anyway. In today's society, many people are getting married at later ages, or perhaps remarrying later in life and potentially creating a blended family. Any time two people are coming together having accumulated their own individual assets, or are coming from an unequal financial position, or especially when the union will create a blended family, it truly is prudent planning and risk management to have a marriage contract (or a cohabitation agreement, if choosing to live together instead of marriage). This legal document sets out what is hers, what is his and what is theirs. It identifies which assets and debts belong to whom, and it can even specify what fair amounts of things like spousal support might be in the event of relationship breakdown. If you are a business owner, whether it be a family business or one you solely own, a marriage contract is your way of maintaining the autonomy of your business. Without it, your spouse may gain ownership rights simply due to marriage. In the event of marriage breakdown, your business could be at risk without that contract.

Very importantly, if you are creating a blended family, a marriage contract can also help protect your children. It is your way to ensure that what you bring into that marriage is what you will leave your children in your estate; without such a contract, those assets you may have intended to be for the benefit of your own children could instead become assets of your new spouse who, rather than remembering your children in his estate, might leave it all to his own children. No matter what the scenario, if you've worked hard to build some wealth on your own, then you need to protect those assets—and your wishes for them—if you're merging your finances with someone else's.

Marriage contracts or prenuptial agreements (the official name depends on your jurisdiction) aren't a negative thing, especially if partners have children from previous relationships or have unbalanced assets. They are smart and prudent tools to protect yourself, and potentially your family too. To be enforceable, they need to be fair and both parties should have independent legal advice before entering into such a contract. These agreements are also a great catalyst for starting open, frank discussions about money. You may just find that these conversations, as difficult as they may be to start, can actually bring you and your partner closer together. Not only can they help the two of you identify and align your financial goals, they may also help initiate deeper discussions about planning for your future, for your retirement together and/or for your estate. And they'll certainly help to prevent the financial friction that causes so many relationships to implode later if money matters are avoided completely at the start.

INSURANCE: MANAGING YOUR RISKS

Protection is also about understanding and managing your risks. Certainly, expect the best; but prepare for the worst. Insurance is one of those things that you hope you never actually need but that you sure will be glad you have if you do need it. When Leslie's car was stolen, the claims manager of her insurance company said these magic words: "You don't have to worry, you have a great policy." In just one claim, they paid out to her more than the total of all the insurance premiums she had paid over the previous sixteen years she had been with that insurance company. She was able to move forward and replace the vehicle with no fuss and no worry. Having a great insurance policy made a world of difference. And that was just for a car.

Now, imagine finding yourself in a position of having to make a disability claim. In this case, we are talking about your health, your well-being and your ability to sustain an income—even your ability to keep a roof over your head and food on the table. The risk of being unable to work due to disability is far greater than the risk of dying prematurely. And yet, so few people make sure they have the right protection in the event they can't work because of a personal health issue. Especially in that position, you would want to hear the words, "You don't have to worry, you have a great policy."

Unfortunately, not all insurance policies are made equal; not all policies are "great." The largest differences in quality of coverage for disability, life and critical illness insurances are the differences between personal (private) insurance you buy on your own versus the coverage you have through your employer, or even through insurance you may have linked to liabilities, like a mortgage. We will talk more about creating financial independence later, but it does come down to having an income stream. If you have an income, you have choices. And not only do you have choices, you also have the ability to pay for your lifestyle. If you don't have an income stream that covers, at a minimum, your basic cost of living, it will be a challenge to be secure financially and impossible to achieve financial independence.

For couples, if one person becomes disabled and the other has an income, it may be possible to get by on just one salary. But if it is not enough to get by, how can you bridge the gap between that one person's income and what your household needs? For single people, of course neither of these scenarios is an option. If you are a single woman (or could be again someday), all the financial responsibility is on your shoulders. If you can't work, how are you going to pay for the roof over your head and putting food on the table, let alone any additional medical costs? There is no one else to provide for you and no one else to protect you, so you must protect yourself. It is essential to understand your risk in the event that you can't work and don't have a backup source of income.

Disability Insurance

According to research conducted by RBC Insurance, the probability of incurring a total disability that lasts longer than ninety days during your working life is as follows:[14]

Age 30:   54%
Age 40:   45%
Age 50:   33%

If you are disabled, and especially if you are single, aside from your regular financial obligations, you are likely to need in-home help. In fact, according to Statistics Canada data from 2006, 60 percent of disabled people need help with daily activities, such as walking, cooking, cleaning, and/or personal hygiene.[15] A single person will need to pay for that help and home care by herself. Less than 10 percent of disabilities are caused by accidents such as injuries at work or motor vehicle accidents;[16] most disabilities are caused by a health issue that results in an inability to work. A period of disability can be any length of time. For a fifty-year-old, the average length of a disability is 3.1 years.[17] But this is just an average, there are those who are deemed disabled generally until normal retirement age of sixty-five. Would you have enough financial resources to cover an extended period of time with little or no income and possibly higher expenses?

The risk of being disabled is real. There are countless stories of disability leading to financial ruin. That may sound melodramatic but, unfortunately, these stories are all too true. Imagine if you couldn't earn your income. Imagine having to draw on savings earlier than planned and what that would do to all your hard work toward your goals. Imagine losing out on your largest savings years (those years closest to retirement) and the impact that would have on your long-term finances.

Part of protecting yourself is making sure you are covered in the event that you aren't able to earn an income due to a disability. If you have benefits at work, there is a good chance you at least have some sort of disability insurance; however, it may not be enough to cover your needs fully, and it is almost certainly not as robust as personal coverage you can acquire yourself. For instance, to keep premiums low, some employers offer long-term disability insurance that will provide disability income for only two years, whereas your own personal policy may cover you for the duration of your disability. And most importantly, if you are insured only through your employer and you change jobs, you may lose your coverage. Not only that, but should you have an illness and lose your employer's coverage, you may not even qualify to buy new personal insurance at that time to replace it.

Again, not all insurance is created equal. Ask some questions to understand what your coverage includes. Is the income before tax or after tax? How long does coverage last? Is this coverage adequate? If you are self-employed, as many women are, can your business continue on without you? If it can't, or if it can but not at a rate that would continue to support your living expenses, how else can you bridge that gap? For many people, looking into private disability coverage is the right thing to do. It is an expense and, quite frankly, no one actually likes paying their insurance premium each month. But, rest assured, if you experience a disability, you will be glad you made the investment to protect yourself and your financial future.

Health and Long-Term Care Insurance

Even if you never become disabled, insurance can play an important role in protecting your financial security and maintaining your financial independence later in life. Leslie recalls an event that her team hosted a few years back, where the guest speaker was talking about retirement lifestyle—you know, things like what your vision is for retirement and what you foresee yourself doing with your time. But the speaker also asked the audience what their number-one retirement concern was. Almost everyone in the room put their hand up to agree that their number-one concern was their health.

Generally, the people who are most concerned about their health in later years are those who are solely responsible for themselves, as the troubling questions become: "If I can't care for myself, who will? If I have high health care costs that I can't afford, is there anyone to help?" This is a tremendous worry of particular concern to women;

as we pointed out earlier, our longer life expectancy means that we will likely be single at some point late in life, even if we are in a committed relationship now. Whether there isn't anyone else to help look after you or you simply don't want to be a "burden," it pays to plan for high health care expenses and/or long-term care costs you may incur in retirement. Unless you have sufficient means, long-term care insurance may be the only way to ensure you can afford the quality of care you would choose for yourself.

The first general criterion of whether you can afford the cost of care is the income level you are planning for. If your retirement plan is well-funded and you are planning for an income level that, later in life, would more than cover the costs of long-term care of the quality you would like and in the community you would choose to be in, then you don't really have to worry as much. If your resources for retirement are a little tighter, then the backup plan becomes selling any real estate you own to provide for housing and care in your later years, provided you aren't planning to leave that asset as a financial legacy. However, many people are choosing to rent in their retirement years, for the benefits of being able to close the door and travel without the headaches of owning a home, for the predictability of expenses (the roof is no longer your problem) and to free up equity for their retirement years. Even if they have the money to do that and their retirement is comfortable, they have no real estate to convert to cash and, therefore, there is no backup plan in the event of declining health.

Whatever the scenario, it may be wise to look into long-term-care insurance. Should you find yourself in a position of requiring some level of care—whether that be in your own home, in a retirement home or in an assisted living or a long-term care facility—each week the insurance company will send you money to help cover that cost. Like disability insurance, long-term care insurance is a living benefit. It pays you to live. Achieving financial independence is about having income streams that cover a comfortable life. And in retirement, that means being able to rely on income streams you still have even though you aren't working. Insurance fills that gap when we can't be sure we can do it ourselves.

It Pays to Start Early

Ardelle shopped for and negotiated long-term care insurance when she was thirty. When she became a teacher at age forty-two, she opted out of her employer's plan, even though it was equivalent and comparable in price and coverage. If Ardelle changed school boards or left teaching, she would be that much older when having to renegotiate an insurance policy, so it would be more expensive than what she already had. The younger and healthier a person is when they arrange insurance, the lower the premiums.

Life Insurance

Finally, let's talk life insurance. Life insurance is there to protect those we love from financial hardship in the event of our passing; and it is there to protect us in the event that someone we rely on financially passes away. For the married couple, life insurance is a means of providing a lump sum of cash for things like covering off any debts, helping make up for the spouse's lost future employment or pension income, or paying funeral expenses. For a single person, whether or not you need life insurance depends on whether there is anyone who is dependent upon you; children, for instance. How much will your children's education cost them if you are not around to help see them through the schooling? Or you may have other family members relying on you, such as aging parents or disabled siblings. If your assets less your debts aren't sufficient to cover those costs, then life insurance is an option to fill the gap.

Life insurance is also there for the business owner. If you have a business partner, if something were to happen to her, would you need an influx of cash; for instance, to buy your partner's ownership stake from her estate? Will the business continue to be a going concern without her, or without you? If not, insurance is a critical piece to ensure that one partner does not lose her livelihood should the other partner pass prematurely.

NOT ALL INSURANCE IS CREATED EQUAL

As discussed, not all disability insurance is of equal quality; coverage and cost can vary widely depending on whether the policy is private or through your employer, among other things. And the same is true of other types of insurance. For example, life insurance premiums through your employee benefit plan or purchased through your financial institution to cover the mortgage can look highly attractive initially; however, as time goes by they can end up costing you far more than if you had purchased quality private coverage earlier instead.

If life insurance is provided by a group plan, such as through employee benefits or an association, premiums may increase at short intervals, usually every five years. With private policies, you can lock in your premiums so that they don't change for ten or twenty years, or even for your lifetime. Sure, your employer- or association-based coverage may be very inexpensive to start, but it can become very pricey over time.

Mortgage, credit card and line of credit insurance, sold by financial institutions, have similar drawbacks as you age. Furthermore, with these types of insurance your premium is set based on the full amount you initially borrow, not on the amount you owe at any given time—and the payout you receive declines as you pay off the principal. For example, let's say you purchase mortgage insurance at $XX.XX a month to cover the total amount you borrowed, which is, say, $300,000. Fifteen years later, you might have only $20,000 left to pay down your mortgage, and that's all your mortgage insurance would cover you for at the time, but you would still be paying a premium of $XX.XX every month. Steadily high premiums for declining coverage is not a good value proposition for you!

The point is, it pays to know what you are paying for and what your choices are. The ins and outs of specific policies are complicated and beyond the scope of this book. If your financial advisor integrates insurance needs into your overall plan, she will be able to provide guidance and recommendations, as would an insurance broker.

In summary, there are some very important points that do need to be made about insurance in general:

- An insurance policy is best designed specifically for your needs. You want the insurance you have to match the risks you want protection from.

- Understand the difference between your coverage through work and any personal coverage you might purchase for yourself. You may be able to get better coverage on your own for not much difference in cost.

- Your need for insurance may change over time. Sometimes this means you no longer need the coverage, or sometimes the purpose of the insurance changes. For instance, your mortgage is paid off, so your life insurance that covered your mortgage may turn into coverage to protect a loved one.

- Part of the financial planning process is about assessing risks and assessing what the risks to your plans are. Insurance should be part of the conversation and part of the overall strategy to protect your ability to achieve your goals.

PROTECTION IS A PERSONAL THING

Protecting yourself is really about protecting your income streams, which may also help protect others you love and are responsible for. As much as possible, you must ensure that you have sufficient income throughout your lifetime, not only to get by and keep you going, but also to keep yourself comfortable in the lifestyle you have chosen or planned for yourself. There are risks that some people are willing to take, whereas others would say, "There is no way I'd take that risk." For instance, there are those who would say, "Well, if I have health issues and I become dependent on the government to care for me, so be it." Others would say there is no way they would want to be in sub-sidized long-term care. They want the highest-quality facility there is, and so they will make sure they can afford it, even if it means buying some insurance to make sure it happens.

Protection is a series of personal choices about what risks you are willing to take, and which ones you aren't. Some ways to protect yourself, like being informed, are generally low-cost or free. In fact, many times, simply an investment of your time makes a big difference in protecting yourself and your financial interests. Other types of protection may have a cost, like an insurance premium. The big question is, if you don't have a way to provide your own protection, can you afford to take the risk or not?

How protected is your goal of being financially independent? Review the following list and see how many statements are true for you.

- I have completed my financial inventory.

- I update my financial inventory regularly and look for changes over time.

- If there is a significant change, I celebrate it when it's a positive change but question it when it's a negative change.

- When life changes, if it involves finances, I try to have a reasonable plan to pay for it.

- If I become disabled, I will have an adequate income to provide for my needs (including being able to save for my retirement years).

- If I have health issues later in life, my financial resources will be sufficient to provide comfortably for me.

- If something should happen to me, those who are financially dependent upon me will be adequately provided for.

- If something should happen to someone I am financially connected to, I will have sufficient resources to make up for that financial loss.

If you can say yes to every one of these questions, you are a financial rock star! If there are any that you are unsure about or to which your answer is no, it is best to invest a bit of time either to research for yourself or to speak with your financial advisor (if he or she provides planning services for clients) to know your options. Remember, there may be risks that you choose to live with. Just make sure you educate yourself about just what that risk is, before you decide you can live with taking it.

PART 3

YOUR POSSIBILITIES

CREATING FINANCIAL INDEPENDENCE

Chapter 8

IT'S ALL ABOUT MULTIPLE STREAMS OF INCOME

So far, we have talked about all the foundational elements that would give you financial security. We covered the importance of building your financial confidence, of being informed about your finances, of having a plan and keeping focused on it, of having a budget whereby more comes in than goes out (and using that surplus to build wealth), and of protecting yourself and your family. These truly are essential building blocks in giving yourself the opportunity to achieve financial independence. Without them, your financial house is built on shaky ground.

Ultimately, financial independence is about providing for yourself a lifetime of reliable income that will comfortably support you and allow you to focus on what matters most and what brings you joy. When you have income, you have choice. An income gives you the ability to spend money doing those things that you enjoy and more options to look after yourself over the course of a long retirement, including the ability to afford the care you want for yourself in later life.

Many people say that having wealth is what you need to be financially independent, and there are hundreds if not thousands of books, articles, speakers, financial professionals and firms that advocate building wealth. However, it doesn't end with accumulating substantial assets—wealth itself isn't the answer. For instance, imagine if you own a home in Toronto, Vancouver, London, New York or Tokyo. If someone owns a detached home in any of those cities, you would think it fairly safe to say that the person should have substantial wealth; however, it is possible that this extremely valuable asset can't easily be turned into an income. That person may have lots of wealth, but she certainly doesn't have financial independence if she doesn't have other assets that can provide a sufficient income. In this case, she is wealthy, but she is house rich and cash (or income) poor.

Financial independence is the result of having sufficient assets (wealth) in forms that can be relied upon to generate the income you need to maintain your lifestyle for your lifetime; or, put another way, to retire comfortably and remain that way. The real trick is, over your working career—as you live within your means, spend less than you earn and invest the difference—your investments build wealth that you can easily eventually turn into income. It is the reliable income generated from your wealth that gives you financial independence.

YEARN TO EARN

Your biggest asset is your ability to earn an income. Intuitively this makes sense. If you have an income, you have the ability to at least cover the costs of your basics in life. The more income you have, the more choice you have and the more ability you have to live comfortably. As you move to later stages of life, transitioning to retirement or into retirement itself, the wealth you have built using the income you earned during your working career needs to generate an income sufficient to sustain that comfortable lifestyle, whether that comfortable lifestyle for you, after tax, costs $50,000 a year, $100,000 a year, $150,000 a year or more—and it needs to last a lifetime. It takes careful planning and forethought to make sure your money will last as long as you do.

In most cases, we all start with one source of income—employment (or proceeds from your own business). During your working years, your goal is to not spend all that income; rather, you need to ensure you are saving and investing a portion. This stage of gaining wealth is referred to as the accumulation phase. You are building assets using the income you receive during your working years, either from employment or from your own business. Ideally, the investments you make will grow and will build still more wealth for you and, therefore, result in more income for your future.

It's easy to float along through life if you are feeling financially secure because you have regular employment income complete with benefits and maybe even the odd bonus or commission. You can count on that paycheque being automatically deposited in your bank account every couple of weeks, you know how much it will be and, if you keep working hard, this may continue for a very long time. But don't allow yourself to be lulled into complacency by the regularity and reliability of your employment income. First of all, there's the chance that you could lose that job, even through no fault of your own, and then what? How would you replace that income? But more than that (and more to the point of this chapter), you don't want to feel so sure about your financial situation in the present that you neglect to think about the future. Instead, take the opportunity to use this regular and reliable income stream to build other sources of income for your retirement.

EMPLOYMENT INCOME: YOUR SPRINGBOARD TO OTHER INCOME STREAMS

To achieve financial independence, the goal is to use your working income or other cash inflows (such as bonuses at work or family inheritances) to generate, ideally, three income streams in the future. If your primary, or only, source of income in your working years is employment income, it can be tough to imagine where else your money might come from, but try to think outside the box. In fact, we will give you the first one: If you are working, you most likely are building future government benefit entitlements (we'll be talking a lot more about this income stream in Chapter 9; for now, just know that it is a natural offshoot of your employment income—another stream you can count on). Depending on your faith in your government's ability to provide those benefits when your turn comes, that will dictate whether or not you want to count this income source as one of your three. If you are already retired or close to retirement, then it is probably fairly safe to count on government benefits. If you are about ten years or more away from retirement, you may want to see if you can build three other streams of income on your own, and then government benefits become your bonus. We'll let you choose.

Consider what other income streams you could add while you are still working, or how you could convert that single major source of income into three or more income streams in retirement. For example, save part of that single stream of employment income every paycheque and start investing to grow your money; over time, doing that can convert your salary into additional investment income down the road. Or start a business on the side. Even if it's just part-time, it will supplement the income you get from your employer, making it easier for you to build wealth and perhaps setting yourself up for a new career path in retirement. The point is, if you are entirely or almost entirely reliant on employment income, you need to start thinking long-term about the money you make day in and day out and how best to put it to work for you.

THREE'S THE CHARM

By the time you reach retirement, which is known as the decumulation phase (when you start to draw income from the assets you have built throughout your working life), your wealth should comprise income-producing assets such as traditional investments (stocks, bonds, mutual funds, etc.), pensions, real estate and/or business ventures. As you know from the previous section, we advocate using your working years to build wealth that will create at least three different streams of income for your retirement, thereby also minimizing risk. That recommendation is based on observation: Leslie has found that diversification—the number-one risk-management strategy for investing—applies to income sources as well. The more income sources you have, the more you are diversifying and, therefore, the more you are reducing your financial risks later in life. The greater the number of income streams available to you, the more reliable your retirement income will be.

If you create a situation like that for yourself and one source of income stumbles—for instance, your rental property goes through a lengthy vacancy period or the investment markets have a bad year—it's possible in those years to draw more from another source of income. When the situation resolves itself, you can rely once again on the income source that faltered after it rebounds, and potentially use it to help replenish the one you had to rely on more heavily for a time. However, if your retirement income streams consist only of your government benefits and rental income, for example, and there is no rent coming in for several months, then where else are you going to get income from? Having multiple income streams to rely on not only helps to supplement your pension money, it also helps to smooth out the ups and downs of the markets, the economy and your investments, thereby creating a more stable, sustainable and predictable retirement income for you.

We know that for a single person, creating three income sources may sound challenging, but it is not as difficult as you may think. You may even be well on the way to multiple streams of income already. Consider this list of potential sources of income to draw on in retirement:

- Employment income (if you decide to keep working even part-time)

- Investments (including RRSPs, RRIFs, TFSAs and non-registered accounts)

- Employer pensions

- Government pensions and benefits (CPP and OAS)

- Annuities (which you can purchase using a portion of your savings or investments to provide a guaranteed income for life)

- Real estate (rental income)

- Business income (from your own entrepreneurial venture that you can start or continue in retirement)

- Insurance with income options

For most people, the first major source of income on the path to financial independence in retirement is government benefits. You can probably rely on the Canada Pension Plan and Old Age Security pension (assuming you qualify for them) for a stable source of income for the rest of your life, but for many women, that won't be enough to afford them the lifestyle they want in retirement. What is your second income stream? What is your third?

IF YOU HAVE JUST TWO SOURCES OF INCOME

Having just two sources of income in retirement is not uncommon; in fact, many people find themselves in this situation. Generally, the two income streams they have are government benefits and their own investments. If you have a defined-contribution pension plan through work, this applies to you; it is simply money in an investment account and not a true pension. You are lucky if your employer is helping you save for retirement, but the assets accumulated in a defined-contribution plan are subject to the vagaries of the markets and will not necessarily produce a *guaranteed* income for your lifetime; therefore, they are not truly a pension and still just count as investments!

If you find yourself in a position where you are retiring with just government benefits and your investments, it is critical to save more than you think you will need. You can't retire with "just enough" to get you through. You need to have excess savings available to weather life's storms or else you need a backup plan. For those who own their own home, oftentimes it becomes their backup plan. If you don't have a home, now may be the time to explore allocating a portion of your savings to create your own pension plan—some sort of additional guaranteed income for your lifetime (purchasing an annuity, for example, as we'll discuss in Chapter 10). Because your risk is that, if your savings run out, one day you will have only government benefits to rely on—and no one wants to be in that situation.

Another common combination of two retirement income streams is government benefits and a defined-benefit pension plan, the type that guarantees income. That pension is most likely one that was sponsored by your employer, if you are lucky enough to have had that kind of benefit in your working years. On the surface, this arrangement seems great: you have two sources of guaranteed income for your lifetime. Certainly, it is a significant advantage; however, it is also the definition of truly living on a "fixed income." What happens if life changes and you have an extraordinary expense? How are you going to pay for it? With no liquid savings to draw on, the only option available becomes debt. Debt is not something you want in retirement. Therefore, if you are retiring with just a pension and government benefits, you shouldn't spend all of that income. You'll need to save during retirement, so you'll have funds set aside that you can draw on when that rainy day comes.

If you haven't retired yet, start building your third income stream now. It is never too late to start. And when that rainy day comes, your older self will thank your younger self for thinking and planning ahead.

TWO WOMEN, TWO DIFFERENT PATHS TO FINANCIAL INDEPENDENCE

A woman we will call Ria (one of our focus group participants), and Ardelle, are both women who are single and have achieved financial independence. They took two very different paths to success, but both have accomplished it by establishing multiple streams of income in retirement.

Ria

Ria is a retired lawyer. Having worked for the government for a portion of her career, she has a good defined-benefit pension that guarantees her income. She became a widow in her early fifties and is the mother of three adult children. Over the years, Ria worked hard. When her husband died unexpectedly, the life insurance was just enough to pay off her mortgage. Fortunately, her income was sufficient to maintain her family's lifestyle and put her children through school. Unfortunately, it wasn't enough to allow her to save. She didn't pay much attention to the fact that she wasn't saving, but she always knew she would have her pension.

When the time came to retire, Ria had her pension, her government benefits and her house. It was a valuable asset but was costing a lot to maintain and Ria didn't want the responsibilities of a house anymore. Relieved from the pressures of work and of being a single parent, now that her children were grown, she wanted to be able to travel and live life with more freedom. In fact, Ria decided she didn't even want to own a condo—she wanted to rent. To maintain a comfortable lifestyle, Ria needs $10,000 per month after tax, an amount that will increase with inflation. Her pension and government benefits alone simply weren't enough. After selling her house and investing the proceeds, she now has three sources of income— government benefits, pension and investment income—that together generate the income she needs to be comfortable for her lifetime.

But for Ria, this scenario didn't quite fit. As much as the investments should be sufficient for her lifetime, she will most likely deplete almost all of them in her later years. It is very important to her not to be a financial burden to her children and to leave them some sort of financial legacy.

And so, instead of leaving all the investments as they were, Ria decided to add to her pension income by using part of her savings to create her own "pension," allocating a portion of her investments to an insured annuity. Doing this not only provides her with another source of guaranteed income for her lifetime, but it will also allow her to provide a financial gift to her children at the end of her life from the insurance proceeds, even if she spends everything else. Ria's retirement income split now looks like this:

10% government benefits
15% annuity, used to create her own pension (after insurance cost)
40% pension from her work
35% investment income

Her retirement income is well-diversified. She has chosen to guarantee a significant part of that income (65 percent of it with government pension, employment pension and annuity combined) as well as guarantee a minimum estate value for her children. Ria's retirement is well in hand—she has achieved financial independence, despite having been faced with the significant challenge of finding herself suddenly single again and with a family to support.

Ardelle

Ardelle has truly done it all on her own. Like many people today, her career was varied and included numerous professional changes. But through it all, her determination to be financially independent provided the motivation behind many of her decisions. Without a partner, and before she worked for an employer who offered a pension, Ardelle bought her first condominium, became mortgage-free, paid for her M.B.A. and teachers college followed by a year of doctoral studies—and all along the way she managed to invest and travel. A partner never helped her reach her financial goals, it was all on her. A partner would have made Ardelle's life different, but a partner wasn't necessary for her financial independence. Her pension provided some security, but her other assets further supplemented and diversified her income. She didn't rely on either a partner or an employer's pension plan.

For Ardelle, building wealth started with owning her own condo. She soon discovered that the great thing about owning your own home is the ability to leverage the equity and use it to then buy rental properties. That is how, on her own and earning a middle-class income, she retired early, owning the condo she lives in plus two investment properties (at one point it was three). The rental income helps to support her retirement income needs and her love of travel and lifelong learning.

Ardelle made a habit early on of saving a significant portion of her income and setting her priorities accordingly. For a period of time she was able to save her entire salary from her full-time employment, covering all her expenses by working additional jobs and running a part-time health and fitness business. The discipline of saving resulted in an investment portfolio that now provides a key income stream in contributing to a comfortable retirement.

A significant part of Ardelle's working career was spent teaching, which means that a portion of her retirement income is a good pension—one income stream that guarantees part of her income for her lifetime.

Ardelle retired, and she did it early, with four income streams in total:

1. Government benefits

2. Rental income

3. Investment income

4. Defined-benefit pension with guaranteed income for life

LESSONS FROM RIA AND ARDELLE

Don't wait until you hit retirement to discover how many income streams you can scrape together. Building future income streams with intention when you are in your working years can accelerate your financial independence. If Ardelle made it happen all on her own on an average income, then you can too!

Sometimes you just need to "re-jig" your resources. Ria had hoped her pension would be enough. It wasn't. Fortunately, she had accumulated wealth (her home) throughout her working life and thanks to being protected by her husband's life insurance coverage. It just needed to be turned into an income for her lifetime. Without wealth, there is nothing to turn into an income. By rearranging her resources, this single-again woman was able to complete her personal financial puzzle and enjoy financial independence, even though she was unexpectedly doing it alone.

Having multiple income streams provides a real sense of security. Both Ria and Ardelle went above and beyond the recommended three streams of income, with four sources of income each. Their income is diversified and, as such, they don't have to be concerned about the ups and downs of one source. They can sleep at night, confident that their retirement income will support them for the rest of their lifetime.

HOW MUCH WILL YOUR FUTURE COST?

The question we cannot answer for you is how much retirement income you need to have in total, because it is a uniquely personal question. It is one that many people will try to attach a general principle to. You may have heard the rule of thumb that, when you retire, you need just 70 percent of your employment income, on average. And, sure, that's what some people need. But how do you know if you are average? In fact, Leslie would say she has never met an "average" person in her whole career. Rather, each person is unique and their vision of, and lifestyle in, retirement is personal. They may share common interests with others or have similar concerns as other people have, but to attribute a rule of thumb to a real-life scenario is like trying to put a square peg into a round hole. It just doesn't work.

This isn't just some time-occupying puzzle you are trying to conquer, where frustration is the only consequence of not finishing. This is your life! If you are trying to plan for your life using a rule of thumb, and the one-size-fits-all solution that it offers doesn't work for you, you run the risk of not achieving your goal in the end. It may work at first, when you are in the early part of your working career and so much of your life is ahead of you that it is hard to tell how things will unfold. Perhaps you start by saving at least 10 percent of your income (a common guideline). However, as your life evolves—whether you marry or stay single, have children or don't, live in an expensive city or in a rural community, enjoy expensive hobbies or those that cost little—your financial patterns and goals solidify, and the income needed to maintain that lifestyle becomes clearer. Then you can really get a solid handle on how much income you will need to save each year to retire comfortably and remain that way.

Leslie has seen people spend significantly more in the early years of their retirement than they would have dreamed of spending during their working lives. There are others who actually spend very little relative to their working income and wouldn't even come close to spending 70 percent of their pre-retirement income. The answer to how much reliable income you need to maintain your lifestyle and live a comfortable retirement depends on how much the lifestyle you enjoy costs. For some women, that may just be $5,000 per month after tax, while for others it may be $10,000 or $20,000 or more each month. It depends on *you*. We may not be able to answer that question for you, but in Chapter 5 we provided a practical tool to give you a quick idea of how much income you will need to enjoy financial independence.

TWO ENORMOUS CHALLENGES YOUR INCOME NEEDS TO OVERCOME

Whether it is during your working years or in retirement, there are two powerful forces that can negatively impact the money you've worked so hard to earn: inflation and taxes. It is essential to be aware of these forces and minimize or offset them both as much as possible, or else they will certainly erode the wealth you've accumulated all your working life as well as the income you can expect to earn in retirement.

Inflation

Inflation refers to the amount the cost of living increases over time. During one's working years, income usually grows over time as well and, as a result, inflation isn't as much of a concern. If, however, inflation outpaces the increases in your income, you will not be able to be maintain your lifestyle; even when you are working and earning a decent income, inflation will erode both your purchasing power and your ability to accumulate wealth.

Inflation has even more serious implications for the quality of your life in retirement, as the negative effects compound over such a long time. As you recall from Chapter 2, if you were to spend $150 on groceries today, in twenty years at a 3-percent rate of inflation, those same groceries would cost over $270. Will you have enough income in the future to cover the ever-rising cost of living, especially for essentials such as groceries? Be sure to also consider the impact of inflation on the cost of travel, the cost of hobbies and your other interests. The rising cost of health care as you age should be another concern. Health does not tend to improve with age. Procedures, medications and personal care are some additional expenses in your future that you may not be paying for now.

As the cost of living increases, it is essential that your income increases along with it if you want to be able to maintain your comfortable lifestyle for your lifetime! That means making sure your income grows during your retirement years to keep pace with inflation. Government benefits and some high-quality pensions are indexed, meaning income increases to keep up with the rising cost of living. How about your other sources? The wealth you build during your working years, which will eventually be turned into your retirement income, must be sufficient to also keep pace with the increases in your cost of living.

Taxes

The biggest bite out of your paycheque, and the biggest drain on your income over time and on your financial resources overall, is income tax. In fact, for many people, taxes are the largest single expense in their lifetime. Both during your working years and in retirement, safeguarding your income and wealth from tax erosion as much as legitimately possible is key to building wealth and achieving financial independence. More important than what you make truly is what you keep.

When you are single, it's even more critical to manage your savings, investments and income to be as tax efficient as possible. And remember, even if you aren't single now, there's a high probability you will be at some point in the future. So, make it a priority to evaluate tax-efficient strategies to minimize your tax bill, not just today but throughout your life. For example, taking advantage of tax-sheltered savings accounts such as TFSAs, RRSPs and/or RRIFs (more on how to do this in Chapter 11) is key to a tax-efficient investing strategy regardless of your relationship status. Unfortunately, in general, there are not as many tax strategies available to singles as there are to couples, so all the more reason to make sure you are making the most of your employment income—budgeting, saving, investing and planning future income steams—in order to combat the heavy impact of erosion by taxes.

If you are married, the decisions you make and the steps you take together today in managing how you most tax-efficiently save and invest or how your household's retirement income is (or will be) generated, can greatly impact the ability of a surviving spouse to maintain his or her lifestyle for their lifetime. As we said in Chapter 4, you should expect bliss. In fact, retirement planning often assumes life expectancies for both people well into their nineties. But make sure to consider what would happen if one spouse doesn't make it that long. What sort of impact will losing a spouse have on the surviving spouse's income? Income sources that are at risk if you are suddenly single in retirement include government benefits and pensions. Not only might the surviving spouse lose some sources of income entirely, now he or she can no longer benefit from retirement income splitting! There is no ability to reduce the taxes on remaining income. All else being equal, for the same level of household income, a single person generally pays more tax than a two-person household.

When planning for financial independence, it is important for a married couple to ask: In the event that one of us dies, will the survivor's after-tax income be sufficient for continuing to live a comfortable life thereafter? It pays to plan with the awareness that one of you will most likely live for some period of time being single. Planning with a view to the loss of one spouse may not be all that fun to talk about, but it can have a very significant impact on the other person's ability to live a financially comfortable and independent life.

INCOME IS INDEPENDENCE

In seeking to achieve financial independence—whether you are currently single or could be again in the future—the income you earn today from employment and/or from your own business must help you fund your life and lifestyle for a long time. Your working income is the foundation of all the wealth you will build and of all the planning you will do; it's the springboard to multiple streams of income in retirement and the biggest contributor to maintaining your lifestyle for your lifetime. Now that you have an idea of how important it is to use your working income wisely if you are to achieve financial independence, let's make the most of it, putting it to work to establish the foundation upon which you build your future sources of income.

Chapter 9

GOVERNMENT BENEFITS
The Foundation of
Retirement Income

Imagine receiving income that is not only guaranteed for your lifetime but also grows as your cost of living increases. As one looks forward to a "retirement" that could last thirty years or more, any income with those two characteristics is highly valuable. In Canada, your government retirement benefits (namely, CPP and OAS) fit that category. For the vast majority of Canadians, these benefits will form an important part of their retirement income. That's why we say that, in most circumstances, you get to count it as your first of three sources of income.

As with anything that has to do with your long-term financial security, it's important to be informed about the government benefits you will receive in retirement; the decisions you make now and as you approach retirement can have a significant impact on the amount you will receive in the long run.

WHAT IS CPP?

The Canada Pension Plan is a pension that you and your employer (or you and your business, if you are self-employed) pay into over your working years. A percentage of the first $55,900 of your income (the Yearly Maximum Pensionable Earnings in 2018) goes into an enormous pool along with your employer's contributions and everyone else's in the Canadian workforce. It is held separately from other government accounts. It is managed, it is invested and it grows. As of 2018, the maximum benefit someone retiring at the normal retirement age of sixty-five can receive is $1,134.17 per month; this amount is indexed to inflation, climbing every year to stay in line with the rising cost of living.

There is a misconception out there that the CPP is in trouble, and many people question whether or not it will be there for them when their time comes to collect it. Yes, there was a period in the mid-1990s when the CPP was underfunded and was at significant risk, and the memory of that time is what has formed some people's concerns over CPP's sustainability today. However, dramatic changes were made to contribution rates and to how the assets were managed. Those changes have brought the CPP back onto solid ground, where it stands today. Actuaries have deemed that the CPP is well-funded and can be counted on. As long as the government doesn't gain access to that separate pool of assets to fund pet projects or make so-called investments in things that don't actually generate an investment return for the contributors to CPP, our government pension plan is in good shape and can be counted on by millions of Canadians as a reliable source of retirement income.

Your entitlement to CPP is primarily based on three things:

1. the amount of contributions you and your employer have made,

2. the number of years you have contributed and

3. when you start to receive your CPP.

Maximizing Your CPP

Although the amount of CPP you will receive is largely based on a formula according to the three variables above, there are other factors you can control, at least to some degree, to make sure you are getting the most out of this government benefit. Firstly, your income matters; the more you earn, the higher your contributions will be and, therefore, the more you will be eligible to receive in CPP payments. In 2018, the maximum annual pensionable earnings amount is $55,900. If you earn that amount (or more) annually, you are maximizing your CPP contributions for that year. All else being equal, the greater the number of years you have been contributing the maximum, the higher your CPP retirement benefits will be.

It's very important to know that if you either worked less or stayed home for the purpose of looking after your children when they were under the age of seven and, therefore, didn't contribute to CPP at all during those years or you made low CPP contributions, you can apply to have those years removed from your CPP calculation under the Child-Rearing Provision, thereby improving your CPP income.

Did You Know? CPP Is Also a Form of Disability Insurance.

As much as CPP is considered to be a retirement pension plan, in the event of significant long-term disability, a disability pension may be available to you as income even before retirement, as well as to any dependents you may have. Those who experience a long-term disability should apply for CPP disability benefits as a source of financial security during such a difficult time. Similar to the Child-Rearing Provision, those years you can't contribute to CPP due to having a disability will not count against you for determining your retirement benefits.

Timing also matters. You can start taking CPP as early as age sixty or as late as age seventy. If you take it early (i.e., before the "normal" retirement age of sixty-five), your benefit is reduced by 0.6 percent for each month you retire early. Delay your retirement to after age sixty-five, and you'll benefit from a "bonus" of 0.7 percent for each month you defer receiving it. Generally speaking, if you are still working and making a reasonable income, you're probably better not to take CPP early unless there is a mitigating circumstance, like you need the additional income to be able to fully pay off your mortgage before you retire. Ultimately, when you opt to start receiving CPP benefits is a personal choice and the best time to start taking CPP is based on your personal circumstances.

Let us be clear—your CPP entitlement is based on you and no one else. As much as the maximum benefit for CPP is $1,134.17 per month as of January 2018, the only way to know how much you can expect your CPP income to be is to call Service Canada and ask. It doesn't matter what your friend receives, or what your co-worker says, or what assumptions may be made—only calling and asking will give you certainty. So, when it comes to planning for your lifetime of income, or actually deciding when to start taking CPP, make the call.

Depending on the circumstances and decisions you are facing, here are two questions you can ask or modify, depending on your personal circumstance:

1. If I continue working and contributing at the same rate I am today, and I retire at age _____, how much will my CPP be when I retire?

2. If I retire at age _____ but delay taking CPP to age _____, what will my benefit be?

The answers to these questions will be far more valuable to you than any rule of thumb you have heard, read about or been advised based on.

Leslie has seen a wide range of answers to these questions. In one case, someone retiring in her mid-fifties found a difference of only a few dollars a month between if she were to start taking CPP at sixty or to wait until she's sixty-five—based on that woman's personal situation. If the difference is literally only a few dollars a month, the decision is easy: take it at sixty. However, the answer is not always so clear-cut and the difference in the amount of monthly CPP income can be quite significant depending on retirement age. In these cases, running a retirement plan with two scenarios—taking it early, or waiting until after sixty-five—can be very helpful in deciding exactly when to start taking CPP. Every situation is different; knowing the variables and the questions to ask can help you make the best decision for you—and maximize the amount of CPP you receive from the government every month for the rest of your life.

What You May Not Know About CPP

Although CPP is intended to provide you with a reliable pension for life, you may end up with much less than you bargained for, and perhaps even nothing at all. Imagine paying into something for years and years and years and getting nothing out of it. That can happen with CPP. You are forced to contribute 4.95 percent of your income each year, up to $2,593.80 in 2018 dollars. But say a young woman starts work at age twenty-five and contributes the maximum each year. Now imagine that she arrives at the door of retirement, is single and age sixty-four, has contributed $100,000 (in 2018 dollars) of her own money, plus what her employer(s) contributed over her working career, but she passes away just before receiving her first CPP payment. The only money she would ever get out of CPP would be the death benefit, a maximum of $2,500. And she wouldn't even get to enjoy that.

What about people who enter, or plan to enter retirement, married? Imagine that a couple who had both worked and contributed the maximum to CPP retire at age sixty-five, at which point they both qualify for and start receiving the maximum CPP. Upon the passing of the first spouse, in this circumstance, the survivor will receive the one-time lump-sum CPP death benefit of $2,500 but will *not* receive any CPP survivor benefits—because they themselves are already receiving the maximum. That household income will instantly drop by $1,134.17 per month, or $13,610 per year.

If, instead, the surviving spouse's own CPP was less than the maximum before losing their spouse, they would receive a top-up of up to a maximum of $680.50 per month; however, the survivor's own CPP benefit combined with the survivor benefit supplement cannot exceed the maximum monthly CPP of $1,134.17. So, if, for example, the surviving spouse had a CPP income of $900 per month before losing their spouse, the most they could receive in CPP survivor benefits would be $234.17 per month, which would bring them up to the maximum CPP of $1,134.17.

CPP survivor benefits can be of some help in some situations, but as discussed above, if you lose a spouse in retirement, you will also lose at least a portion of your household income from government benefits. Finding yourself suddenly single in retirement can be devastating enough; taking this financial hit will only add hardship to the emotional pain. Being informed about the implications will help you plan ahead for a time when you may be single again.

This little-known "secret" about CPP—paying a lot of money into something that you may get very little back from—has major implications for those deciding when to take their CPP, be they single or not. For some, it can be motivation to take CPP early (a bird in the hand is worth two in the bush, after all!) But if you end up living a long time and spending twenty or thirty years, or more, in retirement, starting CPP after age sixty-five will result in you receiving far more in your lifetime than you ever put into the plan. There's no rule of thumb to go by and no one right answer for everyone. Just be informed, so you can plan for your personal situation and make the most of this important government pension.

WHAT IS OAS?

The Old Age Security pension is a benefit that's paid out monthly to every eligible Canadian over the age of sixty-five. It's paid out in addition to the CPP payment and, like the CPP, it is indexed to inflation; but, unlike the CPP, there is no separate pool of funds that you have been paying into to sustain this benefit. You see, like U.S. Social Security, OAS is paid out of current government spending—it is a government expense. As more and more Canadians retire, and as we live longer, that expense is growing every year. In fact, OAS is the Government of Canada's largest pension program.[18] Those who are retired today, or nearing retirement, probably don't have to worry too much about the security of their OAS pension. However, those who are about ten years or more away from retirement may want to be careful about just how much reliance they put on OAS being there, in its current form, for them. Never mind worrying about whether you can rely on CPP; rather, the sustainability of OAS is what we should be concerned about.

Maximizing Your OAS

The maximum OAS payment, as of July 2018, is $596.37 per month if begun at age sixty-five. Like CPP, this benefit can also be deferred to as late as age seventy, resulting in a higher monthly amount. For each month you defer, your maximum benefit increases by 0.6 percent. Having said that, most people elect to take OAS when they become eligible at sixty-five, unless they are still working or have a significant taxable event such as selling an investment property and would have their OAS clawed back anyway. If you are single, or aren't single now but realize that you might be again someday, OAS is an important element in your overall financial picture. It's important for single women to maximize their OAS benefits because when you're on your own, you need to make the most of all income streams available to you.

OAS entitlement is based on four things:

1. Age—you must be at least sixty-five

2. Citizenship—you must be a Canadian citizen or legal resident

3. Number of years of residency in Canada

4. Income level

For instance, if you are sixty-five years old today, living in Canada presently and have resided in Canada for at least ten years since the age of eighteen, you would be eligible for OAS income. However, be aware that there are other scenarios (particularly around residency); so, like CPP, to better understand your personal eligibility for OAS, it is best to call Service Canada and ask with regard to your personal circumstances.

The fourth eligibility factor for OAS is your income. Although you may be eligible for OAS according to all the other factors, the amount of OAS you receive is income-tested each year when you are receiving OAS. The higher your taxable income in retirement, the less you receive in OAS benefits—therefore, beware the OAS clawback! In 2018, you would be entitled to the maximum amount of OAS if your income is less than $75,910. Above this amount of income, your OAS would be "clawed back" by 15 cents for each dollar you "earn" above this level. Once your annual income hits $123,302 (again, as of 2018), your OAS is fully clawed back, and you do not receive a penny of this benefit.

Now, read this carefully: The OAS clawback is like an extra 15-percent tax. It is a tax that can be managed, and it should be managed. If you plan your retirement income carefully, you can have a lifelong income that will allow you to retire comfortably for your lifetime. Maximizing the government benefits you are entitled to and minimizing the various taxes you will have to pay helps make this possible. Some income streams are taxed more favourably than others and can impact the OAS clawback to different degrees. *When* you start drawing on the various income streams available to you and *how much* you take from each one every year are a couple of the levers that can help you maximize your income in retirement and minimize your tax bill. The less you can legitimately pay in tax, the more income that remains in your pocket—and the more you can leave invested each year to continue to grow and create future income for you. The OAS clawback is a tax that, with proper planning, one can, in many cases, minimize if not eliminate. The ins and outs of how various types of income are taxed and how they impact OAS is beyond the scope of this book. Again, a knowledgeable advisor should be able to help, and, with all things tax, a professional accountant should be consulted.

AND THEN THERE WAS ONE . . .

If you are retiring as a couple, the great news is that not only do you potentially get two CPP and OAS income payments coming into your household each and every month, you also get to split your pension income for tax purposes! What does that mean? Well, assuming your ability to split your income perfectly (that is, you each effectively claim 50 percent of the household income), not only will you pay less tax overall than if one spouse had to claim substantially more income than the other spouse, you also have a much higher likelihood of keeping all of your OAS benefit. Your household OAS clawback zone doesn't start until $151,820, so, assuming perfect income splitting, it is much more likely that a household of two would each get to keep their full OAS benefit. Retiring together means that, so long as there are two of you, you have more opportunities than a single person does to keep more of what you make.

Often when couples plan for retirement, assumptions about life expectancy are that both people will live a long time (into their mid-nineties, at least!). Yet, in reality, we know that 90 percent of women will end up financially responsible for themselves and the average age at which a woman becomes a widow is fifty-six. In reality, one spouse usually lives longer than another, sometimes much longer. And if that is the reality, then it's a great reason why every woman should plan financially to be single—even if she's not. Because if you are planning to enjoy a dual-income household throughout your entire retirement and don't consider the "what if," you could be in for an unpleasant surprise when that second income suddenly goes away.

It's extremely important to consider a potentially single you, and the best illustration is the impact on a woman's finances when she loses her spouse's government benefits. We already discussed how CPP impacts a surviving spouse. With OAS, a person receives the benefit during their lifetime and it stops upon their passing. There is no ongoing benefit for spouses or beneficiaries. Whereas CPP at least has a survivor benefit that supplements income for a spouse who may not already be receiving the maximum on her own, there are no survivor benefits with OAS. Upon the death of a spouse, this represents an immediate loss of income up to $7,160 per year from OAS alone. And if you and your spouse retire at sixty-five and are each receiving the maximum CPP of $1,134.17 per month and one spouse passes away, that is an additional $13,610 (annual maximum of CPP as of 2018) of annual income lost. Just from government benefits alone, you could be looking at a drop in household income of over $20,000 per year. And we haven't even looked at the impact on the survivor's tax bill now that she can no longer income split.

As stated at the beginning of this book, planning financially to be single doesn't mean planning independently from your spouse but, rather, planning in such a way that should one partner find themselves single again, the surviving spouse has the financial resources to remain comfortable and independent. Proper planning ensures that if you lose your spouse, financially you will be okay.

Whether you are retiring single or as part of a couple, your government benefits will likely play an important role in providing the ability to maintain your lifestyle for your lifetime. And if you are single, now or in the future, the quality and dependability of your government benefits make those benefits especially important for your long-term financial security. This is also a stream of income that is guaranteed for your lifetime and automatically goes up with inflation. As women have longer life expectancies and as the cost of living continues to increase, these attributes make this type of income especially important for us. It is also why we automatically count it as one of your three sources of retirement income. For the majority of people, their government benefits may be their only source of guaranteed income for their lifetimes. Some are lucky enough to have another source of guaranteed income—a defined-benefit pension. We'll look at it, along with other types of pensions, next.

Chapter 10

INCOME FROM PENSIONS

If you are fortunate enough to have a pension from an employer, you have a significant advantage toward achieving your financial independence compared to people without one. However, even if you don't have an employer-sponsored pension plan, you can take steps to create a pension-like plan of your own. This may be an even more important consideration if you are a single woman and you have to take care of yourself in your older years. If you are very young and just starting out in the workforce, it may be hard to focus on something as long-term and far out as a pension but, trust us, consider yourself lucky to have this valuable benefit. Stick with us in this chapter, and we'll explain just how important this income stream can be in ensuring your financial security, and even independence.

Imagine, a lifetime of guaranteed income, regardless of how long that is. It comes in like clockwork and—if your pension plan is indexed to inflation (meaning your annual income increases at the same rate as the cost of living)—allows you to maintain your lifestyle. Your employer, instead of you, bears the risk on the underlying investment. Now that is a great source of income and a solid foundation for financial independence.

But not all pensions are created equal, so let's first take a look at the various types of pension plans out there and what they mean to you, before turning to how you can create a sort of pension plan of your own if you don't already have one through your employer.

TYPES OF PENSIONS

There are two main categories of employer-sponsored pension plans: defined-benefit plans and defined-contribution plans. Which one you have could make a big difference to the security and predictability of your retirement income.

Defined-Benefit Plans: You Know What You're Getting

It used to be that nearly every worker had a pension that paid a guaranteed income for their lifetime. A defined-benefit pension plan is just that; you know exactly how much you will receive each month and each year—for life. But times have changed. These plans are very costly benefits for employers to deliver, and many have cut back their expenses by cutting out these types of plans entirely. It is estimated that just 26 percent of workers have a defined-benefit pension plan today, and most of those are government workers and public-sector employees.[19] If you have one of these pension plans, you should consider yourself extremely lucky.

The original type of pension, a defined-benefit pension plan guarantees retirees a certain amount of annual income for their lifetime based on factors such as years of service. You know what the amount will be, how much it will increase each year (if it does) and how much a spouse may receive in survivor benefits (if you have a spouse). That means this income is not only guaranteed but highly predictable, and so, it can form a solid basis for your retirement planning. The gold-plated defined-benefit pension is one that is indexed, whereby the income you receive is promised to *increase* with inflation. This is ideal—a reliable *growing* income stream for your lifetime!

When it comes to pensions, the key word is "reliable." A pension's reliability depends on the quality of the organization that has promised to pay it to you. Today, most defined-benefit pension plans (especially those that go up with the cost of living) are given to public employees, those whose paycheques come directly from government in the form of a salary, or given to government-funded offshoots like teachers and nurses. Those pensions are backed by the government, and the government has the ability to increase taxes to pay for those benefits. These pensions, on the reliability scale, are the most reliable. Yes, it is possible that changes may come to these pensions, but generally for those who are retired or are retiring in the near future, these benefits are as close to guaranteed as one can get. If you have one of these pensions, or you are married and your spouse has one of these pensions, you are off to a great start. You get to count this pension as one of your three income sources in retirement. If you decided to include government benefits as another of your retirement income streams, you need just one more!

Now, what about non-government defined-benefit pension plans? They are still an excellent benefit to have, but many of these pension plans offered by corporations and other private-sector organizations do not offer retirees income that increases with the cost of living (in pension language, it's not "indexed to inflation"). If your pension income does not grow with inflation, you will need to rely on other sources of income to cover the increasing cost of living over time.

The second major factor with non-government pension plans is reliability. There's that word again. Reliability depends largely on the financial stability of the organization offering the pension plan. There are many corporate plans that are reliable; unfortunately, there are also those that are not. Generally, when an employee leaves an organization offering a defined-benefit pension, either in advance of retirement or sometimes even at retirement, she has the option to take a lump-sum value instead.

As a financial professional, Leslie doesn't generally advise people to trade in their defined-benefit plan and take the lump sum (also referred to as commuted value) without really understanding the choice they are making; however, there are a few reasons why you might seriously consider taking it rather than leaving it with your employer and their pension provider.

Firstly, if you are facing a shortened life expectancy. Your defined-benefit pension can be worth a lot of money, especially if you have been with your employer for a long time. Therefore, in the event of a known health concern that means a shortened life expectancy, you may want to take the commuted value of the benefit to use in your lifetime or for your estate.

Secondly, if there are any concerns about the ongoing stability of the company providing the pension, taking the commuted value of your pension as a lump sum and running may be a wise decision. In Canada, just ask former Nortel employees or, more currently, Sears employees. Because what good is a defined-benefit pension plan if five years into your retirement the company seeks bankruptcy protection and you find out the pension plan is severely underfunded, and that the income you thought you could rely on for your lifetime just got cut in half? Or cut out completely. Reliability matters.

Probably the most common reason why people decide to take the commuted value of their pension is for estate planning. Defined-benefit pension plans include a survivor benefit, which continues paying your pension or some portion of it after your death to provide for a surviving spouse. But if you're single and you are retiring with a defined-benefit pension plan, your situation may be a little different; because you don't have a spouse, your pension payments cannot continue in the form of a survivor benefit, either in whole or in part. Unless you choose a pension option with some sort of guaranteed minimum number of years your pension will pay out, there may be nothing left for your beneficiaries. This can be particularly challenging for a parent who wants to leave an estate for her children. It is also one of the reasons why people take the lump-sum value instead—to at least have the opportunity to leave a financial legacy should something happen to them, instead of this potentially large asset having $0 value for the people or the causes that matter most to them.

You really have to understand the pros and cons of taking a lump sum and be well-informed of the risks as well as the benefits before you make that decision. When it comes time to retire or to change employers, take the time to understand your payout options for your pension so you can make an informed decision.

Another Reason Why Married Woman Should Plan Financially to Be Single

Don't rely on your spouse's pension. If you become widowed, generally you would receive only 60 percent of his pension. This decrease combined with losing up to $20,000 per year from your spouse's government benefits can have a significant impact on your lifestyle.

Defined-Contribution Plans: You Know What You're Saving

The second, more common type of employer-sponsored pension is called a defined-contribution pension. With these plans, what is certain is the amount you contribute and the amount your employer contributes—not the amount you will receive in retirement. This type of pension is just like having an investment account, and therefore its value is subject to the vagaries of the markets, just like any of your other investments. You bear the risk of the investment value for both sets of contributions. Because it is just like an investment account, if your pension is a defined-contribution plan, you don't get to count this as a separate type of income as you seek to build three reliable income sources for your retirement. It just gets added to your investment portfolio income stream. (We'll talk much more about investment income in Chapter 11.)

Other Employer-Sponsored Savings Plans

Similar to defined-contribution pension plans are other types of work savings plans, such as a group RRSP, a deferred profit share plan (DPSP) and an employee share option plan (ESOP). Sometimes instead of, or in addition to, a pension plan, companies will offer these kinds of savings plans and match your contributions with their own. If your employer is going to match your contributions, make the contributions! Where else will you get an instant 50-percent or 100-percent return on your money? *Always take the free money.* That

instant return will have a tremendous impact on your wealth and ultimately, when you turn it into additional income, it will help you to
achieve financial independence.

YOU CAN CREATE YOUR OWN PENSION

Imagine if you had a guaranteed income for life, and you don't even
have an employer-sponsored pension plan. There are ways you can
make that happen.

The first way to create a pension plan for yourself is by building a
portfolio of high-quality, income-producing investments. If you never
need to touch the principal itself, even to keep pace with inflation,
and the investment income from that portfolio is large enough to last
for your entire retirement, you can reasonably expect to rely on it.
The vast majority of people will need to tap into their capital in the
later years of retirement, and it's relatively rare that the investment
income stream itself would suffice, along with your government benefits, to support your retirement lifestyle; but people who have built
enough wealth to be in this enviable position may not even require a
third income source.

However, most of us will need to create as many income streams
for retirement as possible and, because pensions are one of the rare
sources of guaranteed income, it can be a good idea to use some of
your investment portfolio to create your own. In Chapter 11, where
we discuss investments as a source of income for your lifetime, we
also talk about how investments are your gateway to creating other
sources of income. One way to do that is to take a portion of your
investments and effectively create a pension plan for yourself. The
word *portion* is important because, remember, our goal is for you to
have three separate income streams. We are not suggesting that you
convert all your investments into a self-made pension plan, but that
using a portion of your assets for that purpose can add to your financial security in retirement.

The way to create a pension plan for yourself by using your own
investments is to allocate a portion of your portfolio to purchasing
an annuity. There are many ins and outs regarding annuities, and

far too many people dismiss them completely without actually giving them a fair hearing. But they can be an important element of building financial security and even independence, especially for the single woman who has only herself to rely on. An annuity reduces your risk by converting a portion of your investments, which fluctuate in value with the ups and downs of the market, into a source that provides a lifetime of guaranteed income. A basic annuity is one in which you give a portion of your investments to an insurance company and, in exchange, they guarantee you a set monthly income for the rest of your life. If you live a long time, you receive all your money back and they still keep sending you income, in which case, you win. However, if you live a short time, you won't get back through your monthly income all the money you initially gave the insurance company, and so, in this case the insurance company wins. When looking at a basic annuity, that potential for the insurance company to win is often enough for people to close the door on the annuity option.

But what if there was a way to ensure that you or your beneficiaries would at least get back the amount that you originally gave the insurance company? What if we add what is called a "guarantee pay" option? That option means that, should you live a short time, your beneficiaries will continue to receive the income you had been receiving from your annuity. Combined, for the years you received your income and the years your beneficiaries receive your income, you basically guarantee that the original amount you invested in the annuity will come back to you and your heirs. And even if you live a long time, you will continue to receive your income from the annuity. It remains a guaranteed income for your lifetime.

Alternatively, for those who qualify and for whom leaving an estate is important, you can combine an annuity with a life insurance policy that guarantees that the full amount you give to the insurance company to buy your annuity comes back to your beneficiaries, quickly and tax-free. Again, simply using the term "life insurance" can close minds. But keep an open mind, as this can be a very powerful option, particularly for those who have children and/or are married. During your lifetime, the annuity guarantees part of your retirement income (basically the same as a pension does) for as long as you live. A portion of this income is used to pay the premium on a permanent life insurance policy, which guarantees that you can leave a meaningful financial legacy. Remember Ria, from Chapter 8? This is what she did with part of her proceeds from the sale of her home.

With an insured annuity, you could say you get to have your cake and eat it too! And, if you use non-registered investments to buy an annuity, your income is highly tax efficient. A relatively small part of the annuity income is taxable, and a large part is considered a return of your capital; and, as such, that portion is tax-free. And now, for the icing on the cake: in today's low interest-rate environment, the after-tax annuity income, even after one pays the insurance premium, can be substantially higher than the interest income you would receive from guaranteed investment certificates (GICs) or high-quality bonds. For those who qualify, and in the right circumstances, purchasing an insured annuity can be a great use of a portion of one's investment portfolio.

When it comes to building your own pension, many times there are more considerations and complexities than the investment strategies you may be more familiar with. This isn't necessarily a bad thing. But it is wise to remember this rule: If you don't understand it, or your advisor can't articulate it in a way that you understand, think twice before committing to the building-your-own-pension option. Or at least seek a well-informed advisor who can help you navigate through the choices and pitfalls to make the best decisions for yourself.

Pensions can be a great part of an overall strategy for a comfortable lifelong income. Why just a part of the strategy? You may be thinking, "I have a great pension, backed by the government, so that income will go up every year with inflation. Why do I need to worry about having another source of income?" First of all, you are in an enviable position. Such a pension is a fantastic source of security. But what if you are retired and are, say, seventy-five years old, and something unexpected happens that requires a lump sum of cash such as expensive home repairs? If you retired with just your pension and government benefits (which, by the way, is a common story), how are you going to cover this extraordinary expense? Where is your other source of income if you need it? Or what if your cost of living increases unexpectedly in retirement, and for the long term? Perhaps your pension was sufficient to cover your usual lifestyle comfortably, but then health expenses crept up and suddenly it wasn't enough anymore. With a pension, your income truly is fixed. As great as it is to have your income guaranteed for life, the downside is that there isn't a way to access more from time to time if you need it.

One woman in our focus groups, a retired professional, found this out the hard way. She said she retired early—too early, she came to realize. She thought her pension, which was quite a bit less than her working income, would be sufficient. Unfortunately, it wasn't. Early on in her retirement, a series of expenses surfaced. As a single mom, she still wanted to continue to do things like help her children with their post-secondary education, attend to necessary repairs in order to maintain her home, enjoy weekend trips away with friends and so on. Her income was fixed, so she accessed her line of credit without any extra income available to pay it back. Pretty soon, her home equity was fully tapped out and she was left with two choices: 1) sell her home and rent (giving up the only asset in her backup plan), or 2) get a job and go back to work. Neither option appealed to her, but there were no other choices. She wished she had planned her retirement income better.

THE DOWNSIDE OF A PENSION

Fortunately for Ardelle, she enjoyed her teaching career and wasn't in it just for the pension. But there are others who feel or believe they are "married" to their valuable plan. That is, they are stuck in a job they don't enjoy for whatever reason, but they stay in it because their future independence is so tightly tied to their pension, particularly if they are relying on only themselves financially. They feel they can't leave their job because they would lose out on the future value of their pension benefit, which they are relying heavily on because they didn't build other wealth that could be turned into income. And so, they become a slave to their pension. Imagine, spending at least eight hours a day, five days a week, doing a job you don't like, simply for the income down the road. Is it worth it?

As we've suggested, building three different streams of retirement income, or two sources of income with lots of extra cushion, can help take the pressure off of relying primarily on just one income stream. If you have a pension that guarantees your income, and you also make the effort to build an investment portfolio or create an income stream from a rental property or build another passive income source, it can help loosen the chains. Spending so much of your life doing something that takes away your joy is not a fun way to live. Don't trap yourself by putting all your eggs in one basket. Diversifying your sources of future income not only gives you more financial security, it can also give you more career choices today. Enjoy both your working and retirement years.

Even if you love your current job and you'll be retiring with a pension, potentially even a great one, it is wise to have another source of income to tap into if you need to, or if you want to leave a meaningful legacy for a cause or the people you love. That additional income stream should be something with more liquidity, meaning you can access lump sums to cover expenses if you need to. Having this kind of financial flexibility in retirement does generally mean also having some investments to rely on. Just because you are retired, unexpected expenses don't just go away. Life does still happen. Thankfully!

Chapter 11

INCOME FROM INVESTMENTS

Just as our employment income helps us build entitlement to government retirement benefits in the form of CPP, it is also our means to saving and creating a future income stream from financial investments. Those who achieve financial independence don't spend every cent they make—they choose to live within their means, not only building the capacity to save, but building wealth by turning those savings into investments! Simply saving won't be sufficient to keep pace with inflation. To turn your employment or business income into an asset that starts working for you, your savings must be invested.

Financial investments—like GICs, mutual funds, exchange-traded funds (ETFs), stocks and bonds—are the first type of investments that people usually make. There are many books and other resources available that focus on investments, so we won't go into the details of each type here. We'll focus instead on the strategy you can apply to turn your investments into income and achieve financial independence as a single woman.

Financial investments may eventually provide the income you need for your lifetime directly; or they can be a gateway to building other wealth in the future, if you use a portion of those accumulated financial assets to invest in other assets, like real estate or a business, or to buy yourself a pension (in the form of an annuity) if you don't already have one. Just as having employment income gives you the choice to build financial independence through saving and investing, having investments gives you the choice to build a variety of other income streams to support that independence. We've already covered converting some of the money you've invested into an annuity, and we will get to another type of income-producing investment, specifically real estate, in just a bit.

In the beginning of this book, we talked about practical challenges to achieving financial independence—having enough wealth that you can turn it into an income stream to last what may be a very long time; having that income increasing as the cost of living increases; and, very importantly, being tax efficient. We'll say it again: more important than what you make, is what you keep! These challenges are especially difficult for single people. One set of government benefits, one potential pension and, in retirement, no ability to split income! In retirement, with very few exceptions, for the same level of household income, a single person will pay more tax than a couple. For many, the right types of financial investments held in the right accounts can be a big part of the solution to minimizing the impact of taxes and making the most of your hard-earned money.

BUILDING WEALTH

When initially getting started, and often into one's forties, the point of saving and investing simply tends to be to build wealth. During this early phase, it is primarily about gaining as much as you can—this is the time when you convert part of your employment income into even greater assets by carefully and regularly investing. That's why it's called "building wealth": you're leveraging the money (employment income) you already have and turning it into even more money (investment income) by investing it in such a way as to experience rates of return sufficient to grow it. At some point a portion of this wealth may be used to finance short-term goals, such as a sabbatical or more education to support a career change. But primarily, this wealth you are building is for the long term—for supporting that potentially very long phase of life during which there may not be any income from work, or, if there is, it may be just a small amount from doing something of interest or to stay busy.

One of the common regrets we heard in our focus groups was from women who hadn't put that little bit away from an early age. Because they couldn't put a lot away, they didn't get around to even getting in the habit of putting a little away. Those who had made the effort to save and invest from early on were definitely way ahead of their peers who started later. The women who started early were in a position to think about and debate whether or not they should retire early, whereas those who started late were still having to work, not only to an average retirement age but, in some cases, into their seventies. They are working because they have to, not necessarily because they want to.

That said, it is never too late to start saving and investing. Starting today, whether you are in your thirties, forties, fifties or even your sixties, will have more of a significant beneficial impact than if you waited until next year. The longer you have your money invested, the greater amount you will have to rely on in your later years. Table 11.1 illustrates the difference in wealth at age sixty-five, after investing $10,000 per year earning 6 percent per year, starting from different ages.

TABLE 11.1: Time Can Be on Your Side

Age investing begun	30	40	50	60
Investment value at age 65	$1,114,348	$548,645	$232,760	$ 56,371

Time is your friend and will work to your advantage. The earlier you start saving and investing, the better off you will be because the longer your money will have to grow, thanks to the power of compounding. The more money you have at retirement, the higher the sustainable income that can be generated from those investments, allowing you to have a more comfortable retirement.

TURNING INVESTMENTS INTO INCOME FOR YOUR INDEPENDENCE

As concerns about retirement start to set in, generally in one's forties or fifties, the focus needs to shift from simply accumulating as much as you can to ensuring you are actually on track to accumulating enough assets by the time you retire to provide sufficient income to support you for your lifetime. And as you progress closer to that magical date when you can say goodbye to work and hello to financial independence, actually turning these savings into a sustainable and predictable income in retirement becomes paramount.

The wealth you work so hard to build during your working years can eventually provide you with two types of income. The first type is the growth of capital. The more you are able to accumulate, the higher your investment income. A 6-percent return on $100,000 is $6,000. A 6-percent return on $1 million is $60,000! That return, that growth of your capital, is money you didn't have to earn by working—your investments worked *for* you.

Let's assume your investments grow $60,000 in a given year. You could take that $60,000 as income, add it to your other income sources, and hopefully between all your sources of income, after taxes, you are comfortable for that year. The challenge with this is, what if that $60,000 return isn't guaranteed? What if it is subject to the ups and downs of the investment markets? It means you can't necessarily count on that $60,000 each year. Some years, it may be negative $60,000! Then what will you do? You may have to eat into some of your capital in lean years in the markets, and that may mean less income available to you down the road.

The second type of income that is possible from investments is the income those investments pay. Imagine building a portfolio of financial assets that actually pay you an income, an income that you can use *without* having to touch the capital. Regardless if your return is positive or negative in any given year on your capital, it doesn't matter if it's only the *income* those investments pay out that you use. We are going to focus on two specific types of income characteristically produced by some investments: interest and dividends.

Interest is paid on investments in debt (bonds). For instance, when you buy a GIC you are "loaning" money to a bank or other GIC issuer. In exchange, they guarantee your capital back at the end of a set time frame (say, five years), and along the way they will pay you interest income. Since GICs are guaranteed to certain limits, they are considered very low risk. Very low risk means low return (interest), but interest is income and can be used in retirement.

Dividends are the other source of investment income. Dividends are the type of income paid to those who invest in dividend paying stocks. When you own a stock (a.k.a. shares or equities), you own a piece of a company. You share in the benefits of its growth, and you share in the risks of its struggles. As a company thrives, its sales increase and so does its efficiency and its profits, so the value of your investment increases. As the company increases its cash flow and pays a portion of that cash flow out to shareholders in the form of dividends, you enjoy that income stream. Over time, as that company continues to grow and increases its cash flow, it may increase that dividend. For an investor who is still building her wealth, that growing income stream can be reinvested for more shares in that company, which in turn provides higher future income; or it can be used to invest in something different that can provide additional income. For those who are retired, that income can be enjoyed during a phase of life when you need it to come from something other than employment. Not only is it income, it is potentially a *growing* income stream that helps you keep pace with inflation. A growing income stream helps you maintain your lifestyle for a long time.

Let's illustrate. For the sake of round numbers, let's consider a $100,000 investment today in a stock currently paying an annual dividend of 3.5 percent. If that company grew their dividend at 5 percent per year on average, your dividend income from this investment would grow as shown in Table 11.2.

TABLE 11.2: Power of Dividends That Grow

	Current	5 Years	10 Years	15 Years	20 Years
Dividend income	$3,500	$4,467	$5,701	$7,276	$9,287

Now that growing income can help you overcome a lot of the challenges of achieving financial independence.

QUALITY MATTERS

In reality, it is not uncommon for people to retire with hundreds of thousands, or even millions, of dollars of investments and, for a variety of reasons, to ultimately use all three types of income—capital, interest and dividends. No matter which of these you rely on, quality matters. Quality matters when you know at some point you will need to access a portion of the capital, or when you are relying on the income that flows from that capital. You want to be reasonably confident that your money will continue to grow so that the capital will be there when you need it in the future. When it comes to the income, whether it be from interest or dividends, you want reasonable assurance that income will be paid. This means: beware of getting greedy with institutions that pay a substantially higher interest rate or with a company that pays an exceptionally high dividend. If the rate being offered is significantly higher than the rate being offered by that company's peers, it can spell trouble—it can be a sign that a company may need to cut its dividend or default on its interest payment. That higher income is actually a means of compensating you for taking higher risk. It potentially means a decreasing income for you! That is the opposite of what you need to fund a long, active and sustainable retirement.

Stick with a portfolio of good quality investments. For those with the appropriate risk tolerance, a combination of good quality companies that ideally grow their long-term value and pay dividends, along with bonds or GICs, can create a reliable income over time. It is essential to develop an investment strategy that focuses on providing a reliable income, while participating in the gains of investing and minimizing loses. Your comfortable retirement depends on it.

YOUR INVESTMENT STRATEGY: SET YOURSELF UP FOR SUCCESS

One of the things we heard from numerous single women in our focus groups was that having to make investment decisions—and a fear of making a bad decision—held them back from making *any* decision. Often this indecision led to not doing anything, which meant not actually having their savings grow! Imagine, saving a significant amount of money over the years, but not making an investment decision and therefore missing out on any sort of return. This kind of indecision and, let's face it, paralysis, is often the product of a number of factors in combination. Does any of this sound familiar to you?

- **No vision:** Not having thought about what you are really saving and investing for, what you want to achieve financially or who and what matters most to you.

- **No plan to make it happen:** Not knowing how much you need to save, what investment return is needed to achieve your vision (if you do have one) or the steps you need to take.

- **Lack of knowledge about investing:** Not feeling informed or confident in your own level of financial knowledge, or not having the right professional advisor to help you.

- **No time:** Simply not having enough time to focus properly on an investment strategy and on investment decisions.

Developing a clear, simple investment strategy can help you avoid these problems, all of which are common challenges for a single woman who has only herself to rely on to achieve financial independence. It can all feel very overwhelming and intimidating, but it doesn't have to. Your investment strategy doesn't have to be complicated, and you can get help from a financial advisor to create the one that's right for you.

Investing with a purpose, with a goal in mind, and having confidence that the investment strategy you are using is designed to help you reach your goals over the long term, may give you enough of a catalyst for making the necessary decisions. As in all things, making choices that can move you forward may involve having to endure a temporary step back from time to time (for example, short-term declines in investment value) before you are back on track and on an upward trajectory (and enjoying investment gains). But there is no opportunity to make progress toward financial independence if you don't make any move at all.

Regardless of the specific investment strategy you choose and the specific types of investments you make, simply having a plan will help you avoid some of the most common investing mistakes. The following are broad guidelines and general principles for successful investing:

- **Avoid going to cash in a panic:** When the markets start to drop and stocks decline in value, emotions can cause us to sell our investments for a lower price than we paid for them. And if that's not bad enough, once someone has gone to cash in a panic, when they finally bring themselves to invest again, they often buy back those same investments at higher prices. This is exactly the opposite of what you should be doing to make money in the markets over the long term.

- **Stick with quality:** Buy the names you know—the companies whose products you use and that have withstood the test of time. Around the edges you can have a little fun; risk a little mad money on the lesser-known, riskier investments if you like, but there is no need to gamble with your future.

- **Buy and hold, but don't ignore:** There is often a need to sell some or all of an investment and replace it with another to protect the value of your portfolio. All organizations go through struggles. Some companies that we thought would be around forever ended up failing (Nortel is just one example). Markets and economies go through phases. Buying into the market and staying invested (buy and hold) is usually the best strategy, although sometimes your investments will need to change. You can outsource these decisions of what to own and when, but what you can't outsource is being informed. If you choose to outsource the investment decisions, have regular contact with your advisor to stay informed about your investments and their progress to making your goals happen.

- **Know what you are buying:** If you don't understand it, or your advisor can't explain it in language you understand, don't buy it.

- **Divide into portions:** There are many different types of investments and no one investment will be a silver bullet to your financial independence. Rather, a proper portfolio can and should be built utilizing diversification, a combination of different types of investments. A quality portfolio that is well-diversified is the first step to success; that means not only holding different kinds of investments (GICs and bonds as well as equities, for example), but also investing in different regions of the world (Canada, the United States and global investments). When one category of your investments does well, another will lag. When one category is down a lot, the others will hopefully help offset those losses, so you won't feel nearly as much pain as if everything you had was in one disappointing investment. Diversification is the primary way you can manage risk.

LADIES, WE HAVE AN EDGE

Yes, there are lots of challenges that come with being a single woman trying to manage your finances on your own. It can be a lot harder to reach the goal of being financially independent when you are doing it by yourself. But did you ever consider that you may have a hidden advantage simply because you are a woman? Some of our general tendencies and characteristics can be incredibly helpful in the world of investing. In fact, Fidelity Investments analyzed eight million client accounts in the United States and found that women, on average, actually outperform their male counterparts, achieving a higher rate of return.

Fidelity's analysis showed that, on average, women outperformed men by 0.4 percent annually.[20] On the surface this may not seem like much, but if you consider two thirty-five-year-olds with total investments of $100,000, at sixty-five the woman who returned 6.4 percent would have about $68,700 more than the man who averaged 6 percent. Where this really matters is turning that extra $68,700 into a lifetime of income. At what is considered a sustainable withdrawal rate of 4 percent a year in retirement, that $68,700 edge translates into an annual income that is $2,740 per year *more*. This is definitely an advantage!

The same Fidelity research found that not only do women on average outperform men when it comes to investment return, we also save a higher percentage of our paycheques—9 percent versus 8.6 percent. Fidelity combined both the higher savings rate, and the higher return, and calculated that a woman starting to save and invest at age thirty on a salary of $75,000, at age sixty-seven would have almost $200,000 more than a man starting out at the same age with the same salary.

What is it that makes women such successful investors when we choose to invest?

- **Women are more inclined to be planners:** Planners tend to think about the big picture, investing with purpose and a long-term view. Investing with a long-term view makes you less susceptible to "going to cash in a panic," one of the most common investor mistakes, as mentioned above.

- **Women are more patient:** Fidelity found that women trade less. In fact, in 2016, men who made trades in their accounts made 55 percent more trades than their female counterparts, on average. The patience to buy and hold an investment is linked to the long-term view and in practice means women are at less risk of selling low and buying high—the behaviour that is the exact opposite of successful investing!

- **Women tend to invest, not gamble:** What this means for investing is that women don't tend to chase the latest high-risk investment that their friend told them about. Rather, women tend to invest in higher-quality investments, diversify their portfolios and, overall, take less risk.

So, ladies, we encourage you to make full use of your advantage—plan, have a vision for your future and invest to make it happen! Your financially independent future self is depending on you.

USE YOUR ACCOUNTS WISELY

So far, we have ignored the very real challenge of tax. In Canada, we face very high taxes, whether it be on what we earn or on what we consume. One of the best tools we have to manage both our tax today and our tax tomorrow is the type of account we choose to use when investing.

The tax implications of using various types of savings accounts are a major factor in determining the best investment strategy for you—what types of accounts you use to accumulate your retirement savings, and what types of accounts you invest in and withdraw from in retirement. To achieve a lifelong income, you need to use your accounts wisely. The primary considerations are: What taxes are payable as your money grows? How is your money taxed when it is withdrawn?

When we come to tax, we have all been conditioned to "defer, defer, defer" and to believe that the Registered Retirement Savings Plan (RRSP) is the ideal vehicle for doing that. After all, an RRSP allows you to reduce your taxable income to pay less tax now, and possibly even receive a tax refund; save in an account that lets your money grow tax-free; and then pay the tax way down the road, in retirement. For some people, this strategy can work out well if your tax rate is at a lower rate in retirement than it is in your working years. However, for others who have planned for and achieved a more comfortable retirement, that deferred taxation can bring a nasty surprise. You arrive on the doorstep of retirement with lots of savings in your "retirement" account and you start to withdraw the income you'd planned for, then you do your taxes in the first year and say, "Oh wow, I have to pay *how much*? But I'm retired!" Not only that, but as you go through retirement you are forced to take more and more out and, therefore, have to pay more and more tax on those withdrawals, which are taxed as the highest tax type: income.

This frustration was expressed by more than one person in our focus groups, and Leslie can attest they aren't the only ones who feel it. If you aren't retired yet, take note: Just because the word "retirement" is in the name, it doesn't make the RRSP your *only* choice of account for retirement savings. If you are going to have the ability to have a tax-efficient income in retirement, your RRSP may be *one* of the accounts you choose to invest in, but it shouldn't be the *only* account.

It is best to consult with your accountant and your financial advisor about the specific strategies and account types that will best suit your personal situation, but for reference purposes, we will outline the major account types for you.

Registered Retirement Savings Plan (RRSP)

As we outlined above, contributing to an RRSP allows you to save on the tax you pay today when you contribute to the plan, and allows your money to grow tax-free within your RRSP account; but you pay income tax on all withdrawals when you take your money out to provide you with retirement income. Saving before-tax dollars is a significant advantage. Say you are in the 40-percent tax bracket. If you save $10,000 in your RRSP, you don't have to pay tax on that $10,000, saving you $4,000 of tax up front. It is much easier to save if you don't have to pay taxes first! Say that over time those savings grow to $30,000. Along the way, you haven't had to pay any tax on the growth either. But when the time comes that you need to take that $30,000 out of your RRSP, it is then taxed as "income." Cash flow that is classified as "income" for tax purposes attracts the highest tax rates. Say you are still in the 40-percent tax bracket; then, after tax, you have just $18,000 available. Now, if you are drawing income from your registered account in retirement, you will most likely be doing it from your RRIF rather than from your RRSP, but the tax impact is the same (see below).

Locked-in Retirement Account (LIRA) or Locked-in RRSP (LRSP)

These accounts are just like an RRSP in that money invested in them grows tax-free. However, the money that goes into locked-in accounts comes from a pension plan, generally when you leave an employer and have money in a pension plan that you take with you when you leave. You cannot withdraw money from a LIRA or LRSP before retirement, nor can you contribute or save directly into this account, but you can invest the money held in it. When you reach retirement, the money in the LIRA or LRSP is transferred into a locked-in version of a RRIF, from which you are then able to draw a regular income.

Registered Retirement Income Fund (RRIF)

This is what your RRSP turns into once you are retired and drawing income from your retirement savings. You can choose to convert your RRSP into a RRIF at age fifty-five or older (probably once you are retired), and you have to convert it when you are seventy-one. Once you have a RRIF account, you are required to withdraw a minimum amount every year. That amount is a specified percentage of the total value at the close of the last business day of the calendar year. As you age, the percentage you are required to take out increases. Just like withdrawals from an RRSP, as outlined above, income from a RRIF is subject to tax based on what tax bracket you are in.

Locked-in Versions of a Retirement Income Fund (LRIF or LIF)

A locked-in Retirement Income Fund (LRIF) and Life Income Fund (LIF) are basically identical. Regardless of the title, a locked-in retirement income account is just like a RRIF, but in addition to there being a minimum you have to take from this account, there is also a maximum you can take. This maximum means this account is less flexible in retirement than your RRIF account is.

Tax-Free Savings Account (TFSA)

In Leslie's opinion, for every Canadian aged eighteen and older, this is the most valuable type of account there is for saving and investing! Yes, you save to your TFSA with after-tax dollars (that is, you have to pay tax first and then save), but those savings are able to grow tax-free and when you take money out of your TFSA you don't have to pay any tax. This can be an advantage when "life happens," especially if you're already in retirement and living on a limited income. Imagine that you need to renovate your bathroom, repair a roof or buy a car, or an emergency happens and it's expensive. If you are in the 40-percent tax bracket and need $25,000 for that extra expense, from a RRIF you would have to withdraw over $41,000 to get that $25,000. From a TFSA, you would just need to withdraw the exact amount you need: $25,000. A dollar in a TFSA is worth far more than a dollar in an RRSP, LIRA, RRIF or LRIF.

Non-Registered Accounts

A non-registered account is simply an account that isn't "registered" with the government for tax purposes; it is a "regular" investment account that has no tax advantages and to which no complex rules and regulations apply, as they do to RRSPs, RRIFs, LIRAs and so on. Unlike an RRSP, you pay taxes on your income and then save into this type of account. As your investments grow, you pay taxes on the dividends and interest earned, as well as on any net realized capital gains (gains less any losses) in the year you realize them (sell). The ins and outs of taxation of a non-registered account are complicated and beyond the scope of this book. Suffice it to say, how investments are taxed in a non-registered account can have a significant impact on your tax bill, not just during your working years but also during your retirement years.

Don't Lose in OAS What You Gain in Investing

The taxation of investments in non-registered accounts is especially important for the single woman who wants to maximize her Old Age Security benefits. Different classifications of investment income (such as interest, dividends, return of capital) are each taxed differently and can have a significant impact on your OAS benefit. In fact, in some cases, simply changing investment types in your non-registered account can mean the difference between receiving all your OAS or having a portion clawed back. The best advice: speak with your accountant or a knowledgeable financial advisor who will be able to provide guidance specific to your personal circumstances.

A non-registered account can be your gateway to making investments in other types of income-producing assets. For instance, it is here you may build the wealth that at some point you may use a portion of to invest in real estate or a business or to buy your own tax-efficient pension in the form of an annuity. Taking money out of an RRSP or a RRIF to make such investments would be exceptionally expensive in terms of tax, whereas taking from a non-registered account is far more tax friendly. Just like a dollar of savings in your TFSA, a dollar saved in your non-registered account is more valuable than a dollar in your RRSP.

Using your accounts wisely is complicated and, unless you are an accountant or knowledgeable in tax-related issues, it is advisable to get professional insight into the best accounts for you to use for your personal situation. A few general points of observation and opinion:

- Use all three—TFSAs, non-registered and registered retirement accounts: those who retire with a well-balanced mix of all three types have great flexibility as they look to create a lifetime of tax-efficient income.

- If you have just an RRSP, you will need to save far more for the same after-tax income than if you also had sizable non-registered and TFSA accounts.

- In lower-income years, prioritize saving into your TFSA and non-registered accounts. Build RRSP room and use it in your higher-income years (higher-income years mean higher tax rates and thus higher tax savings when you save into your RRSP).

- With an RRSP the goal is to save during your higher-income years and pay tax on withdrawals from your RRIF (or potentially your RRSP) in low-income years.

- Remember—an account doesn't have to include "retirement" in its name to be a retirement account!

- If you decide that you would like to invest in other assets beyond financial investments (such as real estate or your own business), your non-registered account is generally the first account you would draw on to make those other investments.

Very importantly, for the single woman, using your accounts wisely is especially critical because a single person doesn't have the ability a couple does to split income in retirement in order for each person to pay lower tax rates on the average income. Not only will a single person pay more income tax for the same level of household income in retirement, she also has a harder time avoiding the Old Age Security clawback—effectively, an extra 15-percent tax! Whether it is income from financial investments, or income from other ventures, know the tax implications and structure your income as tax efficiently as is reasonable. Remember, just as important as what you make, is what you keep!

Chapter 12

REAL ESTATE
A Great Foundation

Owning real estate is a huge, long-term commitment and, therefore, isn't necessarily the best investment for all people. In fact, many people will choose not to participate in the real estate market at all. However, it is considered to be one of the greatest ways to build wealth, and investing in real estate can be a great way to diversify your assets beyond the financial markets. It takes time to see the returns, but as mortgages get paid down, large gains can be made over long periods of time as property appreciates. Not only that, but real estate investing is an amazing use of someone else's money. You use the bank's money to build your own personal wealth! Imagine, you put 20 percent ($100,000) down on a $500,000 property and the bank lends you $400,000. Five years later, at a 5-percent average annual return, that property is now worth $638,000. That is a gain of $138,000 in five years. But wait, you actually put down only $100,000 and the rest was the bank's money. Your $100,000 of equity became $238,000 in five years, and that doesn't even include the additional equity you've built by paying down some of your mortgage during that period. That's pretty good!

Not only has owning real estate traditionally been a great way to build wealth over time, home ownership is also uniquely fulfilling and psychologically motivating. When it comes to the daunting task of achieving financial independence (especially challenging when you are on your own), that is a powerful combination. Owning a home not only meets your own basic needs for security, safety and shelter, it can also help fulfill your need for personal esteem, as owning your home provides an incredible sense of accomplishment.

DO THE DOLLARS MAKE SENSE?

The start of the chapter showed the upside of using real estate to build wealth. But when it comes to real estate, whether it is your own home or a rental property, you have to be able to pay for the related expenses and be prepared for the financial risks. The mortgage, utilities, property taxes and maintenance costs are just a few of the expenses you could have. Can you cover all these costs (which typically increase over time) and still save money and live life? If the real estate you own is your own home, do you have savings to cover the mortgage for a period of time if for whatever reason you don't have an income? If it is a rental property, can you carry it for a period of time if you don't have a tenant paying you rent? There are so many potential situations to think about and make sure you're covered for. Real estate can be a great wealth builder, but it generally requires a large amount of debt to finance the purchase, at least initially. Careful financial management is key to making it work and ensuring you are prepared for surprises.

Aside from issues with financing, as well as legal considerations and tenants if you own a rental property, there are the ups and downs of the market to consider. Over the long term, real estate, like many investments, has a solid history of gaining in value. However, just like other risky investments, it can go down in value over short periods of time. Just look at what happened in some regions of the United States in the financial crisis of 2008–09. Real estate values plummeted dramatically and took years to recover; in fact, in some places, property values still haven't bounced back to where they were. Think

Canada is immune? Think again. We don't have to look any further than the 1990s in Canada to see an example of double-digit declines that, in Toronto anyway, took over a decade to recover from. Like any investment, real estate prices will fluctuate, sometimes significantly. It's one of the reasons real estate should be a long-term investment.

Interest rates are another real concern for real estate investors. Again, because of the high levels of mortgage debt most investors have to take on to purchase a home or investment property, they are at risk of becoming quickly overextended if interest rates rise from the present 2018 levels. We may not get back to the double-digit interest rates of the 1980s, but rates are starting to creep back up and even a modest rise in rates could be devastating to anyone who is highly leveraged in their real estate investment.

TODAY AND TOMORROW

As mentioned, real estate is a long-term purchase. Transaction costs are high, the dollar amounts are big and markets may not always go up. The general rule of thumb (yes, sometimes those are okay to use): if you aren't going to own it for at least five years, then don't buy it, whether it's your own home or an investment property. We never know what tomorrow might bring, but holding real estate for the short term, even in a good market, can be a major financial mistake. The high cost of necessary transactions alone (think, realtor costs, land transfer tax, legal costs, moving costs, to name just a few) can wipe out any potential returns or, worse, cause you to lose significant amounts of money.

Leslie once heard of a woman who sold her family home and moved to a smaller house not too far away. But the new neighbourhood really didn't suit her. So, she sold and moved to a place with too many stairs and had to move again. Unfortunately, the cost of three moves in five years completely eroded all the extra funds she had "freed up" from selling her large family home. Real estate mistakes can be costly. Unfortunately, these "mistakes" and frequent moves can easily happen in certain circumstances, such as becoming divorced or widowed, moving for work or retiring. Take your time and do not rush real estate decisions after a major change in your life. Give yourself the best chance of making the right choice and to avoid having to move again soon afterwards. The best advice is to really think through your needs and, if possible, spend significant time in the area you are planning to buy in. For example, can you actually live in a condo and enjoy it if you were used to a house? If you are downsizing, try it out first, if that's an option for you. It may be wise to rent for a year or two and invest the money from the sale of your previous home until you can assess if this kind of radical move is for you. Remember, a property purchase should be at least a five-year commitment.

A good real estate agent can make all the difference. Finding the right realtor is where your journey begins; someone who understands your needs and wishes and who knows the market you are looking to live in. The right professional can help you find the right place at the right time in your life, based on your specific criteria. Not only that, but the realtor should be able to provide you with realistic assessments of the future potential for the properties and locations you are considering to be your home or investment. As much as where you live is a personal decision and based on personal preferences, real estate is a big part of your total net worth. Even if you never plan to sell, it is an asset and it is, therefore, an investment. Chances are that even if you plan to stay in the home you buy forever, you will end up selling it one day or it will be sold as part of your estate to form part of your financial legacy. There can be a lot of emotion tied up in a real estate purchase or sale, particularly when it's your own home, so it's important to keep your financial wits about you and rely on real estate professionals (as well as your financial advisor, banker, accountant and perhaps even your lawyer) to help you make a decision that will be right for your heart, your head—and your financial future.

To find a good realtor, ask friends for referrals to people they had good experiences with. Or attend a few open houses in neighbourhoods you are interested in and see if any of the realtors stand out positively. Not only are you relying on them for their knowledge about the markets, various communities and specific dwellings, you really are counting on them to help you steer clear of mistakes, too. Do your research or a reference check on the person you are considering "hiring" to help you navigate the real estate market.

ALL "BUY" YOURSELF? REAL ESTATE CAN STILL BE FOR YOU.

Many people think that building wealth through owning real estate is out of reach, especially if you have always been single or have become single again. On the surface, a two-person household may seem to have a financial advantage, particularly where there are two full-time incomes. But we want to get the message out that if you are single, you can still build wealth with real estate. Ardelle did it. Leslie knows several women who, like Ardelle, have done it on their own, and many others who became single again who also are successful homeowners.

We talked about it earlier: one of the biggest deterrents to Ardelle as a first-time real estate buyer was other people telling her, both directly and indirectly, that she would not be able to buy property on her own, especially in Toronto—simply because she was a female who had always been single. Quite frankly, it was probably their own personal fear and reluctance that these people were expressing and projecting on Ardelle. Really, what they were saying was that they did not think *they* could or would manage to buy property by themselves and, therefore, she couldn't possibly do it on her own.

One could say the same negative message is all over the media today, with the rising cost of housing especially in urban centres like Toronto and Vancouver. The attitude is, if families cannot afford to buy a home, then single people certainly cannot even consider it. Rising costs are a reality and a challenge, but options exist to make home ownership possible for single people. For example, a single person doesn't need as much living space as a couple or a family does; but if, however, you want a larger property, renting out extra space you don't need is an option to help cover costs.

One very interesting scenario that we are hearing more about is women forming partnerships with others, sometimes their family or friends, to purchase a property. This is a creative solution to a formidable challenge. One piece of advice: If you are going to get into this kind of property-sharing arrangement to invest in real estate, it is very important to have a written legal agreement drafted to spell out all the terms and conditions.

The point is, where there is a will, there is a way. If you want to make owning real estate a part of your wealth-building strategy, you can do it. It may take creativity, hard work and sacrifice, but it can be done. Remember the wise words of Henry Ford: "If you think you can, you will; if you think you can't, you won't."

If you are set on purchasing real estate and doing it by yourself, be prepared to be patient and work extra hard, as Ardelle did. Even though a single person does not need as much space as a couple does, it still can be a challenge on one income to carry even a small home. On the upside, Ardelle did not have to compromise with anyone about where she wanted to buy (downtown Toronto) or about the style of housing (condominium over townhouse, detached house or co-op). She checked out all the options, including properties outside of the downtown core, but she kept coming back to wanting to own a condominium in downtown Toronto. So Ardelle decided to wait so she could save for a larger down payment. All her hard work and long hours paid off, but it took a great deal of energy, dedication and organization, especially since she also managed to lead a balanced lifestyle, have a social life and travel. She was very driven and kept her eye on the prize. But Ardelle didn't stop with just one property. Rather, like many real estate investors, she used her initial investment in her own home as a stepping stone to then purchasing other investment properties to create an income stream that would help her achieve her financial goals and, ultimately, retire early and comfortably.

YOUR MORTGAGE: A NECESSARY EVIL

As we've said before, if you are investing in real estate—be it your own home or rental properties—you will more than likely need a mortgage to finance this very large and expensive purchase. Regardless of which provider or product you choose, the first mortgage statement you receive will make you think there must have been a mathematical error. That was Ardelle's reaction. She could not believe how very little she reduced her mortgage principal during the first six months! She thought that she would have to work until she was ninety to pay off the balance! The longer you "amortize" (period of time you set the mortgage to be paid off), the less of each payment goes to paying down the principal and the more interest you will pay over time. This realization motivated Ardelle to focus on speeding up the process by making a few extra payments and taking advantage of an accelerated payment option. Extra income from her part-time work went toward lump-sum payments directly against the principal, within the prepayment limits her mortgage allowed. These efforts resulted in her original twenty-five-year mortgage being paid off in less than ten years, saving thousands of dollars of interest along the way. Discuss with your banker or mortgage broker what your payment options are, and learn about your possibilities for paying off your mortgage faster. The faster you pay it off, the sooner you will be debt-free and closer to achieving financial independence.

Yes, you need to pay off your mortgage, but it does not have to be a race. You can also slow down the process as life events happen or circumstances change. Situations can occur that stretch your ability to pay your mortgage at times. Some providers allow you to take a break or "holiday" of a few months if you are cash-strapped due to illness or job loss, for example. Just bear in mind that suspending payments, even for a short period of time, will increase the total amount of interest payable in the long run.

Although there may be times where modification of your priorities needs to happen, in the big picture, paying off your mortgage as quickly as possible is very important, particularly in higher-interest-rate environments. Paying off what will probably be your largest debt will mean more money in your pocket to save, invest and put to work in other ways. In Leslie's work she sees many people achieve success by taking different paths. And yet, as different as their strategies often are, one thing they have in common is not just paying off their mortgage but paying it off early. It is one of the most common and most direct routes to long-term financial success.

MAKE YOUR MORTGAGE WORK FOR YOU

Unless the real estate you own can create an income for you, you don't get to count it as one of your income sources for achieving financial independence. A "principal residence," the place where you live, on its own doesn't actually provide an income. You can use it as a "back-up plan," an asset you can sell tax-free without paying capital gains, or access and convert the equity into income or much-needed cash at some time in the future. Or you can use it as a means of providing a financial legacy, if that is important to you. The place where you live may provide the "lifestyle" part of the equation and some financial security, but if you want to stay in it for a long period of time, and well into your retirement, you also need to build wealth that will create an income to help you maintain your home and your lifestyle when you can no longer finance it with employment income.

There are two main ways to turn real estate into income:

1. Access the equity in your own home (the difference between the value of the property and how much you owe on the property).

2. Live the landlady life: have other people pay you for the privilege of living or working in your property.

Tapping into Your Home Equity

One of the ways people access home equity is by downsizing. For example, they sell their principal residence for $1 million, buy a property for $750,000 and now have $250,000 of equity to invest in a way that produces income. This additional income, and presumably lower ongoing expenses, can have a positive impact on your ability to live comfortably for your lifetime. However, a note of caution as you plan to downsize: Leslie has yet to meet someone who actually frees up everything they thought they would when downsizing. You see, many people who downsize see it as a compromise. That is, giving up their larger home and moving to a smaller one, or sacrificing location to move out of the city to where it costs less; in return, many people compromise with themselves, feeling they then deserve a gourmet kitchen or a more luxurious version of that less expensive dwelling. That, along with expenses such as real estate commissions, legal and moving costs, eats into your profit from the downsize.

Don't Move Too Fast

The decision to downsize is a major one. As noted earlier, a bad real estate decision can be an expensive one. To minimize the risk of making a costly mistake, it can be wise not to make the decision to downsize in close proximity to major life events such as retirement, widowhood or divorce. Each life transition brings with it an emotional adjustment, and adding a move can simply compound stress.

Real Estate Investing: Become a Landlady

The next choice is to join the ranks of the true real estate investors, being a landlady who either rents out a portion of the home you live in or purchases an investment property. In either case, you are turning a real estate asset into a steady stream of income. As a landlady, you have someone else essentially pay your mortgage for you by paying rent (that is building wealth) and eventually, once the mortgage is paid off, paying you regular income (an additional income source you can use to live your financially independent life, either before or in retirement). Those are the wonderful upsides. However, real estate investing comes with its own challenges, responsibilities and potential downsides. So, just as with other major life decisions, it is wise to consider all the risks beforehand.

Rental income certainly can provide positive capital growth as well as a steady income stream. However, it is important to consider rental income as extra income rather than a main income source. The property could be vacant while the expenses to maintain it continue or even rise, or you might find yourself with a tenant who doesn't care for your property or doesn't pay their rent! Both situations would reduce your cash flow and add to your expenses.

Beyond maintaining your property and carrying costs (mortgage, property tax, etc.), there are additional expenses involved with
real estate investing. For instance, if using the services of a realtor
or management firm to find good quality tenants, the fee will typically be one month's rent. You should also maintain insurance on
your property, keeping in mind that insurance may not cover dam-
age caused by a tenant. Although such expenses on rental properties
can generally be claimed on taxes, they will not be totally recovered.
Professional accounting and legal advice is strongly advised when it
comes to real estate investing, so that you can protect yourself and
your investment.

Just like any investment, it pays to be informed and do your research so that you understand the landlord and tenant laws in your
district. In some jurisdictions, there are restrictions on how much you
can raise the rent (rent controls), even if your costs may be increasing at higher rates than the rent increase limits. Furthermore, it can
be extremely difficult and time consuming to legally evict a tenant.
Potentially, there can be many months where a tenant is living in your
property, not paying rent, while you go through the eviction process,
which could make you late with mortgage payments. Good tenants
are key to successfully using real estate as a strategy for building your
wealth and diversifying your income streams. Credit checks help, but
be aware that a credit check on a potential tenant does not include the
person's history of rent payments. Someone may choose to pay a cell
phone bill, which affects their credit score, over paying rent, which
does not. In Ardelle's experience, she has found it worth the cost to
use the services of a knowledgeable realtor to assist in finding good
tenants. One month of rent is a small price to pay for this service,
compared with the expense and headache of having a tenant who is
not responsible.

Tenant issues aside, there are other practical issues to consider
before taking on the role of landlady. When you are not available,
who will be responsible to take care of your property and tenants
should a situation arise? If piping bursts or an appliance breaks, the
situation needs immediate attention. If you purchase a rental property in another city or you travel often for business or leisure, you may

not be easily able to take care of issues on site. Is there a company or person you can trust to manage your rental? If "outsourcing" is the route you take, of course you will need to pay for that (so you'll need to factor that cost into your financial planning), and you should have a written agreement that clearly outlines everyone's roles and responsibilities.

In summary, home ownership is not for the weak of heart, especially if you're trying to accomplish this major purchase on your own. So, if owning real estate can be such a challenge, then why would anyone purchase additional properties? Is it worth it? It most certainly can be. But you must do your due diligence. It is wise to do adequate research, both as an investor before purchasing property and as a landlady when choosing tenants, to prevent unnecessary risk and stress.

It all comes back to this investment being an option to build wealth initially plus create income streams later, once the mortgage is paid. Again, it isn't for everyone and you get to decide if it appeals to you. Some people don't have the time, the means or even the desire to be a homeowner, let alone to become a landlady. But for those who choose to invest in real estate of any kind, it can be financially and personally rewarding, as it was for Ardelle. Providing a home for a nice person who will take care of your property while your equity grows can be extremely satisfying and worthwhile. After all, as the saying goes, "Home is where the heart is."

PART 4

YOUR SUPPORT TEAM

Chapter 13

WORKING WITH YOUR ADVISORS

There is a saying that "It takes a village to raise a child." One could say the same thing about achieving financial independence. It may be your journey, and you may be making it on your own, but your chances of getting there efficiently and successfully are higher if you build a team of people who can help you along the way.

Your team may include professionals (e.g., financial advisors, accountants, lawyers, bankers and realtors) and non-professionals—your personal cheerleaders and others whose opinions you value and rely on to help you make decisions. Each of these people can play a different role and may offer you a slightly different perspective. Some of your team may be with you for a long time, and some members may change over time.

Some professionals you choose to work with may have a broad range of knowledge (some financial advisors, for example) and others will have a specific area of expertise (the lawyer you use to buy your home may be different than the one who writes contracts for your business, for example). Each person potentially fills a particular need for expertise, and these experts can work together in helping you achieve your broader goals. In the first chapter we talked about your personal support team and how you can surround yourself with friends and mentors who are positive and avoid the naysayers. In this chapter the emphasis is on how professionals can help you navigate your many financial decisions.

Not everyone needs every type of professional. Some people have the natural interest and inclination to "do it themselves" on matters such as filing their own tax returns, managing their own investments and/or making their own financial decisions. In some cases, doing it yourself is the right choice and can save you money. If you choose to manage some things on your own, be sure to educate yourself and gain as much knowledge in that area as you can in order to reduce the risk of error. And be aware that you don't know what you don't know. The unintended consequences of what you don't know can end up costing far more than the cost of the professional advice and services. Consider that even doctors, dentists and hair stylists who provide their professional services to others rely on their colleagues for their opinions and to help them personally.

A relationship with a financial advisor can be as simple as him or her providing you with investment advice; or it can be a very deep relationship where your advisor is fully engaged in, and committed to, what matters most to you and understands where you have been, where you are today and what your vision for your future is. Whereas many other professionals' roles are quite specific, this vast range of what a relationship with a financial advisor can be led to many questions from the participants in our focus groups. Our intent with this chapter is to help answer those questions about working with a financial advisor and to provide insight from both a financial advisor's perspective (Leslie) and from a client's perspective (Ardelle).

THE VALUE OF ADVICE

First of all, as much as not everyone needs a financial advisor and it is possible to do it on your own and do it quite successfully, the statistics show that those who do work with a financial advisor consistently derive the following benefits:

- They grow more wealth.

- They have more confidence in their financial future.

- They experience less stress.

A major academic research paper by the Center for Interuniversity Research and Analysis of Organizations (CIRANO) looking into the value of financial advice found that after removing all other social and economic factors, the only thing left to explain the difference in the amount of wealth achieved was having financial advice or not, and that those who work with an advisor accumulate significantly more wealth than those who don't. In fact, those who had worked with an advisor for fifteen or more years had accumulated 2.73 times more wealth than a non-advised household.[21]

We have talked a lot about confidence in this book and the importance of building and having confidence. This same body of research by CIRANO found that 56.4 percent of those who received advice have confidence in their ability to retire comfortably. Just 40.8 percent of those who are not advised have confidence.[22] Other research has taken it further and, rather than looking just at advised compared to non-advised households, looked specifically at those whose advice included having a financial plan. Of those with a financial plan, 81 percent feel they are on track financially.[23] Ardelle can attest that she thought she was on track for her retirement, but it wasn't until she actually had a retirement plan that she was certain that her years of hard work had paid off and she could do it, and that she actually had confidence to move forward into retirement knowing she could live the life she'd envisioned and enjoy a life of financial independence.

Having confidence in one's finances reduces stress, as does having a financial advisor who is knowledgeable and who will save you time by doing some of the work for you. Your advisor can help create your financial plan, proactively provide advice and track your progress while making investment recommendations based on your personal tolerance for risk as well as for your current and future needs and goals. An advisor can help you through the ups and downs—not only with investing but also with the many other financial challenges and decisions we all face as we move through life. For those who really wish financial matters could be simple, a good advisor should be able to take what is complex and make it simple for you. Including speaking in a language you can understand. Ardelle found that when she understood the language the advisor used, she was then better informed and more confident when making her decisions.

To help you build more wealth, contribute to you being confident and to take away the worry, your advisor should be in fairly regular contact with you. Ideally you meet with them in person once per year for a comprehensive review, or as needed if life changes or you have a particularly pressing need. In the interim, ask your advisor or potential advisor what their communication process is. Some may have a regular schedule they follow for contacting clients, while for others it may be more of an as-needed contact schedule.

For those who want to achieve financial independence but don't want to do it alone or who feel they don't have the knowledge or inclination to manage it all themselves, an advisor can provide tremendous assistance. The trick for those wanting to work with an advisor is finding the right advisor for you!

A WHO'S WHO OF ADVISORS

There are so many different titles that advisors go by that you may well ask, what's the difference between them all? We wish there was an easy answer . . . there is not. Part of the issue is that many financial professionals do similar tasks but fall under many different designations and titles. At present, the title given to a person in an advisory role can be determined by the firm they work for and is generally one of several available titles approved by regulators for those in an advisory role at that firm. It is important to understand that most advisors have tremendous independence in running their practice. They serve their clients the way they see fit, applying the skills and abilities they personally have into a service offering. This means that not all advisors are the same, and not every advisor will be well-suited to serve all clients, *regardless* of the title the advisor has!

To best answer this question of who's who, and to get to the substance beneath what can be a somewhat arbitrary title, we are going to break financial advice into four general categories under which the services a financial advisor may fall: investments, insurance, financial planning and wealth management.

Investment Management

Investment Advisor, Investment Executive, Portfolio Manager—these are the titles that generally apply to investment management. The advisors who focus in this area specialize in providing investment advice. They manage your investment accounts, ultimately working to help you build your traditional investment wealth. (Traditional investments include those related to the stock and bond exchanges, GICs, mutual funds, etc.) An investment advisor will make recommendations to you, and you decide whether or not you want to take her advice. For those who prefer not making individual investment decisions such as when to buy or sell, a licensed portfolio manager can make those decisions for you. She is able to handle your accounts on a "managed" basis. This means you delegate the responsibility of making day-to-day investment decisions to the portfolio manager who manages your investments within the parameters you agree to ahead of time.

Insurance

Insurance specialists generally sell insurance products (including annuities) to provide protection during one's life and to protect those who are dependent upon that person. Insurance can be a very important piece in providing financial security. Some insurance agents also sell investments under an insurance umbrella (segregated funds). These investments are generally more expensive than traditional mutual funds, as they also provide some protections in investment values within certain time frames. Insurance-based investments can be helpful for estate planning as well.

Financial Planning

Financial planners work with you to develop plans that help you achieve what matters to you the most. Some financial planners simply provide the plan, but they don't sell the investments to make those plans happen. In those cases, the client pays a set "fee" for the specific financial planning service. Some financial planners will also provide the investments recommended for you in the plan.

Wealth Management

Wealth Advisor is a newer title and is bestowed upon those whose firms want their advisors to provide a complete range of services and advice to high-net-worth clients. Wealth management is when a single advisor brings all the pieces together in a more holistic way. Not only does the wealth advisor manage investments, she also manages the financial planning and insurance to fulfill the needs identified by the client's financial plan, which in some cases includes things like tax-efficient income strategies, business succession planning and a variety of other services to meet the specific needs of that particular client. An advisor who truly focuses on holistic wealth management should have deep understanding of the real needs, wants and vision their client has of his or her future.

AS YOUR NEEDS CHANGE, YOU MAY NEED TO CHANGE ADVISORS

The type of advisor you work with may change over time. When you first start out, you may simply need investment advice. As your savings grow and life becomes more complicated (as it often does as we move through the decades), your need for financial planning becomes stronger. As your wealth builds and your needs become more complex, a wealth advisor who brings all the pieces together for you and works with your other professionals (accountants, lawyers, etc.) may be the more appropriate fit.

Remember: just because an advisor has a particular title doesn't mean that it's the advisor's core competence or the actual service they provide their clients. A title is bestowed upon an advisor by their firm. Yes, there are certain requirements for eligibility for the advisor's title, and the advisor must have those qualifications, but it doesn't necessarily mean that it is what they do, or solely what they do. It isn't about the title. It's about what services, knowledge and skills the advisor can provide for his or her clients. How do you find out this information? You ask them. If you do not feel confident that your advisor is best suited to meet your needs for your stage of life, then it may be time for a second opinion.

WHAT QUALIFICATIONS SHOULD MY ADVISOR HAVE?

There are countless designations in the financial world, even more so than titles. There are a variety related to expertise in the area of financial planning, investment management, estates, insurance and so on. Some are country specific, others are global in nature. Two advisors who offer the same services can have completely different sets of designations, and yet both can be well-qualified and knowledgeable to provide the services you are looking for.

The best thing you can do is ask your advisor or potential advisor to explain to you his or her qualifications. The advisor has invested significant time and money in their own education and development, so, no doubt they will be happy to explain what their qualifications are. You can then assess if the qualifications demonstrate that this advisor is knowledgeable about and able to perform the services you are in need of. Follow up by asking why they chose to pursue those specific designations. While there are no clear right or wrong answers, how they answer can certainly offer great insight into the advisor's mindset.

Sometimes people are aware of a designation that is fitting to what they need, but the advisor they have or are considering working with doesn't have that specific designation. If you are wondering why that advisor doesn't have a specific designation you are looking for, ask. You might be surprised at the answer. For instance, Leslie has several designations, but there is a well-known and frequently marketed financial planning designation that she does not have. Although she wanted to pursue it, she was informed that because she had been in the industry a long time, she would first have had to re-write elementary courses taken at the start of her career. Instead of going backwards, she chose to take specific courses that would allow her to actually provide new, meaningful knowledge on practical financial planning matters that clients would benefit from. As part of your interview process, make sure the advisor explains the services they can provide and their qualifications. However, it isn't just about the qualifications, it's also about gaining insight into the person, their mindset, how they think and their personal philosophy.

BESIDES QUALIFICATIONS AND TITLES, WHAT SHOULD I LOOK FOR IN A FINANCIAL ADVISOR?

Just as with any partner, "fit" matters when it comes to your financial advisor. Do you get along with this person? Do you feel that you can tell him or her anything and they will still be on your side and that they will maintain your confidentiality? Do they truly buy into your dreams and your vision for your future? If their job is to help you achieve that vision, they better be genuinely interested in it and want to help you attain it! Do you feel this is a person whom you can trust and who you feel in time will be able to earn even more of your trust? These are some really big questions, and a lot of these answers are going to come from your instincts, especially at the start of a relationship. Only through working with your advisor over time will you gain more confidence and trust in them, and in your choice.

"Fit" should work both ways. What many people may not realize is that just as much as you are interviewing a potential advisor, they are interviewing you. Are you someone they feel they will be able to work well with? Just as not every advisor is the right fit for you, not every client is the right fit for an advisor! Let's be honest, you want the person you are relying on to provide advice to you to enjoy doing so. One way to gauge whether or not you will be a good fit for that advisor is to ask, "For you, what is a good client?" Again, there is no right or wrong answer to this question. Rather, this is a great way for you to get a better understanding of your potential advisor, the type of practice they run, and their mindset and attitude. This particular question is one Leslie has been asked only a couple of times, but as an advisor, in her opinion, it is one of the best questions because it helps both of you determine fit—and fit matters! Hopefully you get more than just technical answers, like how much good clients have in investable assets, and you get responses that relate more to the types of personalities the advisor works well with—and whether they have experience working with people in circumstances similar to yours, such as helping single females.

There are no right or wrong answers. Rather, the answer to any of your questions can give you a better understanding of how your advisor thinks and how they feel. And it is another source of fuel to help guide you and form your instincts, so you can have more confidence when making your decision about hiring a financial advisor.

Some Interview Questions to Ask Potential Advisors

- What services do you provide your clients with?
- Do you provide these services personally, or do you bring in someone else?
- How frequently should I expect to speak with you?
- Working together, what will my total cost of investing and working with you be? (Be prepared—there may be choices for you to make, and those choices may have different costs associated with them.)
- What investments are you licensed and able to use in strategies for your clients?
- What qualifications do you have? (What do the letters after your name mean?)
- Why did you choose to pursue those qualifications?
- For you, what makes a good client?
- What do you believe makes you a good advisor?
- Do you have clients who are similar to me; and, if so, how have you helped them?

DIFFERENT FIRMS FOR DIFFERENT NEEDS: THE CHOICE IS YOURS

There are different types of firms that employ different types of advisors, who offer different investment products and advisory services. Typically, each firm and how established an advisor is will dictate the minimum amount of assets needed to work with that advisor. Although we present the various types of firms as quite discrete from one another, in fact the distinctions between them can be quite blurred, with considerable overlap in the kinds of products and services provided in some cases. Nonetheless, the brief descriptions that follow should give you some idea of the different players in the investment and advisory landscape.

Discount Brokerages

For those who choose to do things themselves, discount brokerages offer low-cost transactions on stocks, bonds and exchange-traded funds (a.k.a. ETFs). For mutual funds there may be some lower-cost versions available, but many times the cost is no different than if you held them with an advisor. Those who choose to invest with a discount (a.k.a. online) brokerage should be knowledgeable and have the interest and time required.

Robo-advisors

Relatively new to the investment management space are robo-advisors, so called because they provide a largely automated (internet-based) service. Complete a questionnaire, pick a portfolio and a robo-advisor will do the rest of the investment work for you. This is a lower-cost solution and fine for investment management, especially for people who are just getting started. What robo-advisors don't do is provide truly personalized advice for you. The requirements for investable assets are very low (potentially as low as $0), but those low minimums may make the costs of having a very small account excessive. Cost is often relative to the amount you are investing. The lower the amount you have to invest, the higher the effective percentage cost.

Retail Banks

For a more personal approach, the first stop is often the bank. All banks have financial advisors in their branches who can help answer some personal questions about investing as well as provide investment solutions. Like robo-advisors, banks generally require very low minimum investments (somewhere around $500). The difference is that the bank will provide some personalized recommendations and some advice around financial matters beyond investment, such as advice regarding mortgages. Financial advisors at the branch level may be able to open very small accounts, but they also are able to provide advice to those with significant assets. At some point, generally over about $500,000 in investable assets, and when the client is in need of a higher level of service (including advanced financial planning and other advisory services), the branch advisor will likely make a referral to an advisor in the bank's wealth management division.

Non–Bank-Affiliated Firms

As you start to increase the amount you have invested, and your life becomes more complex over time, you may search for more specialized investment and financial advice. This can be available at the full-service wealth divisions of big banks, or at independent firms. There are two main categories of these independent firms, and they are very different.

One category is often able to provide only mutual funds and perhaps a limited range of other investments. At such firms, beware of proprietary products! These are products that can only be owned at that particular firm, in which case your investments aren't portable, meaning you have to sell them if you want to leave. Selling these proprietary products to invest somewhere else can result in significant expense. For instance, a mutual fund may have a deferred sales charge on redemption that, depending on how long you held it, can cost you up to 6 percent of your investment value. In addition, there can be tax consequences for selling any investments that are held in a non-registered account.

The second category of independent firms may be able to offer the full spectrum of investments, or at least most of them. Financial planning and wealth management may or may not enter into the equation, depending on the services provided by your individual advisor, and such services may be offered only to those with higher investment values. Minimum investment values will generally be lower for the first group (those primarily engaged in selling mutual funds) than they will be for those offering the full spectrum.

Wealth Management Firms

Then there are the full-service wealth management arms of the major financial institutions. A complete range of services and advice is available for those who need it—not just with regard to investment management, financial planning and insurance, but also estates and trusts services, business succession planning, private banking plus many other areas of expertise to draw on should the client need them. On the other hand, some advisors in these practices may choose to focus solely on investment management. It comes down to the individual advisor you are working with. Wealth management divisions of the major financial institutions have high minimum account values of at least $250,000. In major cities, many established advisors have minimum requirements of $500,000 or even $1 million to work with them.

Portfolio Management Firms

The core competency of these companies is investment management, and the main reason people invest with these firms is for access to proprietary portfolios. Clients invest a minimum of generally $1 million to $5 million, and they invest in the firm's proprietary portfolios, but *not* the type that have deferred sales charges. Many times, these clients hold investments at multiple portfolio management firms. Generally, the client seeks not only financial planning but also sophisticated tax and legal advice from other professionals.

AS A CONSUMER, WHAT PROTECTS YOU?

Sometimes client–advisor relationships don't work out for whatever reason. As mentioned earlier in this chapter, you may need to move on to a new advisor simply because lives change, needs evolve and the "fit" just isn't there anymore. But the sad reality is that sometimes we need to move on for other reasons. As consumers, we need to protect ourselves, and be protected, from the potential failure of the advisor's firm or those advisors who may do wrong.

The first line of protection is to know what kind of firm actually holds your investments and is the custodian of your assets. Is there some level of protection built in that can safeguard your assets? This question speaks to the security not only of the investments themselves but also of your account value in the event of failure of the firm. What protects you? In Canada, the Canadian Deposit Insurance

Corporation protects bank accounts and GICs from failure of the firm or issuer, up to $100,000 per insured category. The Canadian Investor Protection Fund protects accounts at member investment firms up to $1 million per type of account. Find out if your account is covered by some kind of insurance in the event of failure of the firm your advisor works for, and what the limit is.

What rules and regulations do your advisor and the firm have to comply with? And who is overseeing that compliance requirement? Who is monitoring the investments in your account for their suitability compared to your stated risk tolerance and objectives? This isn't necessarily just about ensuring that your advisor does right by you; it's also about ensuring that, as your life changes, your accounts keep pace and change with you. It also is a protection against an advisor who doesn't necessarily follow all the rules.

Especially important when considering small firms, what are the protections you have from becoming a victim of a Ponzi scheme or some other fraudulent activity that results in the loss of significant savings? Unfortunately, if there is one commonality when it comes to Ponzi schemes, they are usually run out of firms where the advisors have the ability to influence clients' statements. Or, if they happen in a larger firm, they usually affect investments that are made outside of the accounts held at the firm and, therefore, outside the purview of organizational compliance and oversight. Whatever firm your advisor is with, or whatever investments he or she is making on your behalf, make sure that person cannot influence your statements. If you are dealing with a small independent firm, ideally your actual account is held with an independent custodian and you receive statements from the custodian firm as well as from your advisory firm so you are able to verify values. For instance, at some small independent firms your advisor may purchase mutual funds for your account from a third party. Those funds would show on statements from the advisor's firm, and you would also receive a statement from the mutual fund company where the fund is held. Something that gives you the ability to verify the value of the account from a reputable source is useful in these situations. Regardless of the firm's size or affiliation, never, ever, make a cheque payable directly to your advisor!

If you have a concern that your advisor has not adequately addressed your needs and questions, or you feel something untoward is going on, the first step is to contact the advisor's branch manager. In Canada, the regulators have spelled out specific requirements and processes for handling client complaints and investigations, which the firm must follow. The complaint process starts with the firm your advisor works for, but should the firm not be able to resolve the issue adequately, they must provide you with the contact information at the next level so you can take your complaint further up the chain. In Canada, we are fortunate that there is significant regulatory oversight focused on the protection of clients.

Ardelle unfortunately had a negative experience the very first time she worked with an advisor. Luckily, she reviewed her monthly statements regularly and asked questions. She quickly realized there was a problem, and when her concerns were not adequately answered by her advisor to her satisfaction, Ardelle filed a complaint and she changed advisors. Her lessons from the experience: First, being informed meant she realized there was a problem quickly before it became an even bigger problem over time; and second, one bad apple doesn't spoil the bunch. Since that first negative experience, Ardelle has had nothing but positive experiences with advisors.

Questions to Ask Yourself About an Advisor

- Do I understand what this advisor is telling me?
- Does he or she speak to me in a way that I like to be spoken to? (Some people complain that advisors are difficult to understand or that they are arrogant.)
- Do I like their responses to some of my "fit" questions? Instinctively, do I like what those answers tell me about this person?
- Is this advisor someone who I feel I can trust with my money, as well as with very personal information and even my innermost fears, dreams and goals?
- Do I like this person, and would I look forward to working with them?

HOW MUCH DOES IT COST TO WORK WITH AN ADVISOR?

The cost of investing is largely a function of the amount of money you have to invest and the type of investments you make. The best way to look at investing cost is to split it into two parts: the cost of the advice and the cost of the investments.

The Cost of Advice

First, as mentioned earlier, there are financial planners who, for a fixed cost, will provide you with a financial plan. They just do the planning work but don't provide investments or ongoing investment advice. The cost of working with an advisor who provides the investments themselves (and potentially financial planning as well) can be driven by either a "transactional" model or a "fee-based" approach. In its simplest form, a transactional relationship effectively means you pay as you go for the financial products you purchase, and these costs usually apply to making the investment itself rather than getting any broader financial advice or services. For example, you do a trade, there is a cost.

In the broader and more inclusive fee-based model of investment advice, you generally pay an annual fee based on a percentage of your total assets under management with an advisor, and it covers all aspects of the management of your accounts including transactions. If your advisor also provides planning services, these are often included in the cost. This fee varies with the amount of assets you have and the scope of services your advisor provides. It is important to note that if your investments are in a non-registered account, this cost of advice is tax deductible.

In the industry, the general rule of thumb for investment advice (distinct from financial planning advice on its own) is that $1 million of investment assets is typically priced in and around 1 percent. Below that, the percentage is more, with the highest fees applying to clients who have less than $500,000 to invest. Generally, only if you have about $2 million to $5 million to invest might your annual cost of advice be lower than 1 percent of your total assets. These are general guidelines. Pricing norms vary by geographic area, and each advisor follows a different fee schedule. For example, an advisor who provides total wealth management may charge more than one who focuses solely on investments.

The Cost of Investments

The cost of the investments you make is another consideration. With stocks and bonds, other than the face value of the specific stock or bond you are purchasing, there are no other significant costs associated with holding these securities (although you will pay for each trade you make if you choose the transactional model, or a percentage of the value of your investment each year if you go with fee-based advice). They may effectively come at a relatively low cost, but the risk and volatility of individual securities can mean they aren't the right fit for everyone.

With exchange-traded funds (ETFs), in addition to the cost of advice (the trade or the percentage fee you pay your advisor), there is an imbedded management expense ratio (MER), an additional percentage you pay each year to hold these products. MERs can range from being very low (approximately 0.10 to 0.25 percent) on what are known as index-linked ETFs (replicating the performance of a major stock or bond index; for instance, in Canada the S&P/TSX Composite), to being about the same cost as a mutual fund for ETFs with complex strategies.

Mutual funds are known today for being a high-cost investment product. The cost (also in the form of an MER) comes from paying professional portfolio managers to invest on your behalf, actively. Fortunately, mutual fund MERs are starting to fall, reducing the cost of holding these products, and ETFs offer a lower-cost alternative in many cases. On average, mutual fund MERs would be 1.8 to 2.6 percent in a transactional account, or 0.75 to 1.5 percent in a fee-based account where you pay separately for advice.

Finally, there are segregated funds. Segregated funds are like mutual funds, but they have an insurance wrapper. This wrapper guarantees things like your investment value over certain time periods, death benefits and the ability to tax-efficiently distribute assets to beneficiaries, in addition to offering some creditor protection. Some segregated funds even offer a guaranteed minimum income for life.

As with all guarantees, there is always some kind of cost. In general, it is fair to say that segregated funds are more expensive than mutual funds. The more guarantees there are, the higher the cost. In fact, it is not uncommon to see the total cost of investing in segregated funds to be between 3 to 4 percent.

Other Potential Costs

Depending on the firm you work with, and sometimes depending if your relationship is fee-based or transactional, there may be other costs to be aware of. These can be administrative in nature, such as an annual account administration charge, or costs for financial planning. In a transactional account, it is common for these to be charged. Within a fee-based account, many times, but not always, these are included in the cost of advice. Other costs can stem from such things as custody charges and safekeeping (charges for actually holding your investments). These are generally charged at trust companies or at some "private wealth" firms.

The Total Cost of Investing

Your total cost of investing is the combination of:
(cost of advice + cost of your investments + any other costs) *plus tax!*

THERE IS NO FREE LUNCH

All investments have a cost whether you invest on your own or with an advisor. An advisor can, and should, fully explain your cost of investing. She will also be able to discuss any alternative strategies and their costs, to verify whether a change makes sense, or to confirm that your current portfolio structure is the right one for you. But to start the conversation, sometimes you have to ask!

To put costs into perspective, the Fraser Institute estimated that the total cost of managing the Canadian Pension Plan is 1.15 percent annually—and that is to manage approximately $300 billion of assets.[24] Cost matters, but value matters more. And only you can answer whether or not you are getting value for what you are paying.

Ardelle feels that, overall, having had professional advice helped her reach all her financial goals, and much faster than she would have done on her own. Even though there was a cost (and those costs were discussed at different times), the real value for Ardelle was in reaching her goals and doing so faster than if she had not had an advisor working with her; so, to Ardelle, the returns were worth the fees. Her advisors offered a wide variety of strategies and investments, many more than she knew about or could access on her own. Practically, those strategies and investments made her plans happen. And, very importantly, as a single person, having a professional as a sounding board was a comfort to Ardelle. Her advisor was, and is, a key member of her team.

Making the decision to work with an advisor or to change advisors is a big one and isn't to be treated lightly. A great relationship can be rewarding and help you achieve your goals. A poor choice can set you back and cause you stress and worry. Consider which services you need and which ones you could benefit most from. Look for the advisor's qualifications to validate her ability to knowledgably provide that advice. And finally, and critically, find the right "fit" and value for your hard-earned money.

Chapter **14**

IT'S TIME TO TALK . . . AND ACT

Women talk with each other about everything. Or do we? Think about it: Have you ever had an open and honest conversation about money matters with a female friend? Can you think of a woman you would feel comfortable enough to talk with about your finances? One of our main goals in writing this book is to encourage women to start conversations with other women about finances, a topic that has been taboo for too long.

We shouldn't fear talking about money. As women, one of our strengths is naturally networking with, and being supportive of, one another. The same support should apply when it comes to handling our finances. There's no reason we can't help each other and learn from each other, celebrating each other's successes along the way. There are so many single women out there in various financial situations and scenarios—why should we all have to go it alone when we have each other? Let's start having the conversation nobody wants to have.

Maybe you are that woman one of your friends would choose to talk with about her finances. If so, listen and make suggestions, but try not to judge your friend's financial habits and situations, especially if she is opening up to you about them in confidence. What may be a wise decision for you may not be the best one for a friend, and only she can truly know this. Your style may not be her style, just as what you perceive as a goal or a success for you may not be one to her. The point is everybody is different, and support is what we all need.

QUESTIONS FOR PERSONAL REFLECTION

But before you can have meaningful, productive conversations with other women about financial matters, be sure you've had an honest conversation with yourself. Know where you stand and where you want to go financially. The following questions will help you reflect on your own situation and spark discussion with your supportive friends, families and mentors as well as with your advisor. You may even choose to record your responses in a personal financial journal. (Remember, writing down your goals and your vision and detailing your financial inventory will give you a greater chance of success.) Think of answering these questions as your first step on the path to your financial independence.

- What do you value?

- In what ways, other than financially, is your life rich?

- What are the relationships, interests and personal goals that bring you joy? Do any of these elements of true wealth come with financial planning needs?

- What do you want your future self to look like? What do you want your life to look like in the future? What's your vision?

- What do you want to change about your finances in the future?

- What do you wish your younger self had known about money?

- What fears do you have about your financial future?

   o What is one thing you can do today to improve your life tomorrow?

   o What other steps do you need to take?

- What financial accomplishments are you proud of?

- If you are currently partnered, how would you manage financially if you were to become single? Are you presently informed about all aspects of your household finances?

- What are your present and future income streams?

- How prepared are you for a financial emergency?

- Have you made a financial inventory?

- Are you prepared financially if you were to no longer be able to work due to health, disability or downsizing at your workplace?

- How well do you understand your pension, OAS, CPP values and the impact each benefit would have on your income depending when you decide to start collecting it?

- Have you called Service Canada to inquire about your government retirement benefits?

- Have you called your company's HR department or pension administrator to find out more about the amounts you will receive in retirement and the various payout options from your work benefits?

- To what extent are you a generous enabler? Is there anyone in your life who is capable (or who should be capable) of supporting themselves and yet you continue to subsidize them financially?

- What talents, hobbies or skills do you have that you could turn into ways to make extra income?

- Who do you admire for what they have accomplished financially?

- Knowledge and action are both important elements in preparing for your financial comfort. Which of these areas needs more of your attention?

- Considering where you are today, what actions do you need to take in order to prepare financially for your future? What is the first step you could start with?

GROUP DISCUSSION QUESTIONS

In the spirit of helping other women and learning from other women by having conversations about financial matters, why not get together some of your gal pals for a book club–type discussion focused on what you've read in *Bank on Yourself*. After all, sharing is caring. You could plan an evening and give it a theme like "Food and Finance" or "Wine with Wealth." However you want to go about it, the questions that follow can help you start and guide the discussion, but of course you'll want to create and include your own.

- What one piece of financial advice is worthy to share with others?

- Regarding financial risks, which ones come to mind, especially for single women?

    o Discuss strategies to manage these risks.

- What are the positive and negative experiences you have had with things like: money, banking, investments, real estate, mortgages, financial advisors?

    o What are the lessons learned from these experiences?

- What savings strategies have you used that worked?

- How have you managed your budget/banking?

- What are the most concerning challenges, especially for a single woman, that involve money either directly or indirectly?

- For those who have a partner in life, as a couple how have you managed money?

    o What strategies worked?

    o What strategies haven't worked?

- What one thing did you learn from this book that may change your thoughts or actions regarding your financial situation?

BANKING ON YOURSELF: SEVEN STEPS TO SUCCESS

As you look to your future with great expectation, there are seven simple steps that will empower you to bank on yourself and achieve financial independence. Remember, financial independence is not only about being financially secure but also about having the freedom to focus on the interests, goals and relationships that bring you joy and fulfillment, both during your working years and ultimately during your "retirement"—whatever that means to you.

Regardless of your stage of life, marital status or current financial position, here are the seven steps to bank on yourself to achieve financial independence if you remain single or become single again:

1. Take your financial inventory (be informed about where you stand financially).

2. Assess your income and expenses.

3. Identify your vision for your future.

4. Put a plan in place to make your vision your reality.

   - Create (or plan for) your three income streams.

   - Protect yourself and your plans.

5. Set your budget: Put your plan into action (remember to balance enjoyment today with being smart about tomorrow).

6. Track your progress toward your goal.

7. Review and repeat the steps above as needed and as life changes.

Very importantly, remember to build your team—the person or people who support and guide you on your journey to financial independence. Even though you may be single, you are not alone.

END NOTES

Chapter 1

1. Nelson, Jacqueline. "Women and Wealth: The Investment Sector's New—and Crucial—Frontier," *The Globe and Mail Report on Business*, August 9, 2014, updated May 12, 2018. (See https://www.theglobeandmail.com/report-on-business/women-and-wealth-the-investment-sectors-new-and-crucial-frontier/article19979192/?page=all)

2. Wang, Wendy and Kim Parker. "Chapter 2: Trends in the Share of Never-Married Americans and a Look Forward," Pew Research Center, September 24, 2014.

3. Myers, Kady. Poverty and Health in Canada: A poverty intervention tool for Nova Scotia, University of Victoria, School of Public Health & Social Policy, September 2014. (See https://www.policyalternatives.ca/sites/default/files/uploads/publications/Essay_Grad_PovertyHealth.pdf)

4. Townson, Monica. "Canadian women on their own are poorest of the poor," Canadian Centre for Policy Alternatives, September 8, 2009. (See https://www.policyalternatives.ca/publications/commentary/canadian-women-their-own-are-poorest-poor)

5. *The Lancet*. "Low socioeconomic status reduces life expectancy and should be counted as a major risk factor in health policy, study says," January 31, 2017. (See https://www.eurekalert.org/pub_releases/2017-01/tl-tll013017.php)

6. Statistics Canada. "Why are the majority of university students women?" December 1, 2008. (See https://www150.statcan.gc.ca/n1/pub/81-004-x/2008001/article/10561-eng.htm)

Chapter 4

7. Nguyen, Linda. "Top reason for divorce? Money, says BMO poll," The Canadian Press, February 12, 2014. (See https://globalnews.ca/news/1144095/ top-reason-for-divorce-money-says-bmo-poll/)

8. Vanier Institute of the Family. "Separation and Divorce in Canada: By the Numbers," December 2013. (See https://vanierinstitute.ca/wp-content/ uploads/2015/10/BTN_2013-12-11_Separation-and-Divorce.pdf)

9. Evans, Pete. "Canadians owe $1.71 for every dollar of disposable income they have—a new record high," CBC News, December 14, 2017. (See https://www. cbc.ca/news/business/debt-income-1.4448098)

10. Marr, Garry. "Seniors in Canada are racking up debt faster than the rest of the population," *Financial Post*, September 5, 2017. (See https://business.financialpost.com/business/seniors-in-canada-are-racking-up-debt-faster-than-the-rest-of-the-population)

Chapter 5

11. Financial Planning Standards Council. The Value of Financial Planning, 2013. (See https://issuu.com/fpsc/docs/value-of-financial-planning)

12. Society of Actuaries. Annuity 2000 Mortality Table.

Chapter 6

13. BMO Financial Group. "BMO RRSP Study: Eighty-nine Per Cent of Canadians Plan to Rely on the CPP/QPP to Fund their Retirement," January 30, 2014. (See https://newsroom.bmo.com/2014-01-30-BMO-RRSP-Study-Eighty-nine-Per-Cent-of-Canadians-Plan-to-Rely-on-the-CPP-QPP-to-Fund-their-Retirement)

Chapter 7

14. RBC Insurance. "Less than 10% of disabilities are caused by accidents, such as workplace injuries or vehicular accident," January 4, 2017. (See http://www.rbcinsurance.com/disability-awareness/causes-of-disability.html)

15. Statistics Canada. Participation and Activity Limitation Survey 2006: Technical and Methodological Report. (See https://www150.statcan.gc.ca/n1/pub/89-628-x/89-628-x2007001-eng.htm)

16. RBC Insurance. "Leading Causes of Disability." (See http://www.rbcinsurance. com/disability-awareness/causes-of-disability.html)

17. RBC Insurance. "Introduction to Income Protection," August 2014. (See http://www.rbcinsurance.com/businessintelligencecentre/file-805839.pdf)

Chapter 9
18. Government of Canada. "Old Age Security—Overview." (See https://www.canada.ca/en/services/benefits/publicpensions/cpp/old-age-security.html)

Chapter 10
19. Statistics Canada. "Pension plans in Canada, As of January 1, 2016," *The Daily*, July 21, 2017. (See https://www150.statcan.gc.ca/n1/daily-quotidien/170721/dq170721d-eng.htm)

Chapter 11
20. Fidelity Investments. "Who's the Better Investor: Men or Women?" May 18, 2017.

Chapter 13
21. Cockerline, Dr. Jon. "New Evidence on the Value of Financial Advice: A Guide to the Research Paper 'Econometric Models on the Value of Advice of a Financial Advisor,' by the Center for Interuniversity Research and Analysis on Organizations," Investment Funds Institute of Canada, 2012. (See https://www.ific.ca/wp-content/uploads/2013/08/New-Evidence-on-the-Value-of-Financial-Advice-November-2012.pdf/1653/)

22. Cockerline, Dr. Jon. "New Evidence on the Value of Financial Advice: A Guide to the Research Paper 'Econometric Models on the Value of Advice of a Financial Advisor,' by the Center for Interuniversity Research and Analysis on Organizations," Investment Funds Institute of Canada, 2012. (See https://www.ific.ca/wp-content/uploads/2013/08/New-Evidence-on-the-Value-of-Financial-Advice-November-2012.pdf/1653/)

23. Financial Planning Standards Council. The Value of Financial Planning, 2013. (See https://issuu.com/fpsc/docs/value-of-financial-planning)

24. Cross, Philip and Joel Emes. "Accounting for the True Cost of the Canada Pension Plan," *Fraser Research Bulletin*, Fraser Institute, September 2014. (See https://www.fraserinstitute.org/studies/accounting-for-the-true-cost-of-the-canada-pension-plan)

TAKE IT TO THE NEXT LEVEL
Bank on Yourself . . . to Achieve Financial Independence

Leslie McCormick is passionate about helping clients achieve financial independence. In her role as a Senior Wealth Advisor at one of Canada's leading wealth management firms, Leslie and her team use a series of specialized tools to create *Your Personal RoadMap*—a customized and individual blueprint to guide you to the life you envision. Wealth is only partially defined by your money; true wealth is also about your life and the relationships, goals and interests that bring you joy.

Your Personal Roadmap brings clarity to the planning process, provides you with a step-by-step plan and allows you to focus on what brings you joy and fulfillment:

- Clearly articulates and plans for your goals.

- Turns wealth into a reliable lifelong income.

- Tracks progress and empowers you to actually turn your vision into your reality.

- Helps you navigate the many financial choices and decisions you have to make in order to enjoy financial independence and *Retire on Your Own Terms.*™

If you are interested in connecting with Leslie, she would enjoy hearing your story. Leslie can be reached at: leslie@plansingle.ca

• • •

Both Leslie and Ardelle enjoy sharing their knowledge and experiences through speaking engagements. Their mission is to help women who are single, or may become single again, develop confidence in their ability to achieve and maintain not just financial security, but financial independence—the higher goal.

Leslie and Ardelle would be happy to engage with your group. For more information about *Bank on Yourself* presentations, please visit us at: www.plansingle.ca

ABOUT THE AUTHORS

Ardelle Harrison is living her dream, happily retired and busier than ever. Her degrees and careers in family studies, business and education helped her learn to create a healthy, active and balanced lifestyle. Her interests include real estate and finance and she is passionate about travel, performing arts and people. Ardelle reached her goals on her own and all by herself. She may be single and solo, but is never alone, thanks to her wonderful friends and family.

ardelle@plansingle.ca

Leslie McCormick is a Senior Wealth Advisor with one of Canada's leading wealth management firms, where she has been advising clients for over fifteen years. In addition to the internationally recognized Chartered Alternative Investment Analyst (CAIA) designation, she holds the Financial Management Advisor (FMA) and Chartered Investment Management (CIM) designations and is a Fellow of the Canadian Securities Institute (FCSI).

Leslie is dedicated to helping her clients realize their vision for the future and throughout her career has taken a keen interest in helping single women, and those who may be single again, be informed and in control of their financial future.

When she isn't working, Leslie enjoys spending time with her family, playing tennis and travelling.

leslie@plansingle.ca